Don’t Be Afraid of the Mainframe

Don't Be Afraid of the Mainframe

The Missing Introduction for IT Leaders and Professionals

Niek de Greef

Don’t Be Afraid of the Mainframe: The Missing Introduction for IT Leaders and Professionals

First edition: 2026

ISBN: 9789083597003
eBook ISBN: 9789083597010

Publisher: Seneqa, The Netherlands

Disclaimer: All company names, product names, trademarks, and registered trademarks mentioned in this book are the property of their respective owners. Use of these names is for identification and educational purposes only and does not imply endorsement by or affiliation with the trademark holders. The opinions expressed in this book are those of the author and do not necessarily reflect the views of any mentioned companies or organizations.

Contact: seneqa.nl

Executive Summary

This book is written for IT executives, enterprise architects, and technology directors who need to make strategic decisions about mainframe platforms. It's equally valuable for CFOs evaluating IT investments, application and infrastructure architects and specialists modernizing legacy systems, and consultants advising on platform strategy. Whether you're deeply technical or business-focused, this book gives IT professionals the essential knowledge they need in a straightforward, low-friction manner, without drowning in unnecessary complexity.

If you are responsible for technology strategy, you've probably encountered the mainframe question: Should we keep it? Modernise it? Replace it? And honestly, who can blame you for feeling stuck? Decades of myths, technical jargon that makes your eyes glaze over, and a frustrating lack of straight talk make this decision unnecessarily difficult.

That's why I wrote this book. To cut through the nonsense and give you what's been missing: honest, vendor-neutral guidance that helps you make the right decision for your organization. Not based on fear or fashion, but on actual business value.

Three Things You Need to Know

The mainframe isn't legacy; neglect is

Here's what surprised me when I started working with mainframes in 1990, and what still surprises people today: mainframes aren't museum pieces. They process 70% of the world's transactions. They handle 90% of credit card payments. They deliver 99.999% uptime.

Modern mainframes support AI, containers, REST APIs, Python, Java, and all the DevOps tools your teams already use. You can run OpenShift on them. You can integrate them with AWS or Azure. The "green screen" thing? That's mostly a myth nowadays.

The real problem isn't the technology. It's organizations that stopped investing in it, let technical debt pile up, and then wondered why it became expensive and inflexible.

Cost is complex—but manageable when you understand it

Mainframe costs confuse people. Licenses with mainframe terms like MSUs, the 4HRA calculation, and the MLC versus OTC models are deliberately opaque and put people off.

Here's what matters: software is roughly two-thirds of your total mainframe cost. Not the hardware, the software licences. Understanding how licensing works is critical. The good news? New pricing models exist that can be competitive with cloud alternatives, especially for new workloads. You just need to know they exist and how to negotiate them.

I have dedicated a chapter (Chapter 15) to making sense of this, because you can't make good decisions without understanding the money.

Doing nothing is the only wrong answer

You have options. You can modernise the platform and applications. This is often the most cost-effective path. You can migrate everything to other platforms. This is expensive, risky, but sometimes necessary. You can take a hybrid approach, keeping the robust core on the mainframe while building new capabilities in the cloud.

What you cannot do is nothing. I have seen organizations postpone decisions for years, watching technical debt compound, costs spiral, and business agility suffer. Some even had to shut down business lines because their IT couldn't keep up.

Whatever you choose, you need to act.

What's in the Book

I have organized the book into three parts, and you can navigate it however suits you best.

Part 1: Understanding the Technology (Chapters 1-8)
What's actually in that big box? How does z/OS work? What about Linux? What languages do people use? I explain the fundamentals without drowning you in jargon. If you're not technical, the reading guide in Chapter 1 shows you which bits to skim.

Part 2: Modern Capabilities (Chapters 9-13)
How do mainframes integrate with the rest of your IT landscape? What does modern development look like? Why is mainframe security still the gold standard? In this section, I show you how mainframes operate in today's hybrid, cloud-connected world.

Part 3: Making Strategic Decisions (Chapters 14-18)
This is the business end. How should your applications be architected? What are your transformation options? How do costs really work? How does cloud strategy apply to mainframes? And what does the future look like?

Questions I Answer

Different readers come with different concerns. Here's what I address:

If you're a CIO or IT executive:
How do I position the mainframe in our overall strategy? What's the real total cost of ownership? How do I build the business case? For investment or divestment?

If you're an enterprise architect:
How do mainframes fit in modern, hybrid architectures? What integration patterns actually work? How do I standardize and automate this environment?

If you're a CFO or business leader:
Why are the software costs so high? How can we optimize spending? What's the ROI on modernisation versus the cost of migration?

If you're a technical leader:
How do I attract young talent to work on this platform? What modern tools exist? How do I implement proper DevOps? What about containers and cloud integration?

If you're an IT professional needing mainframe literacy:
How do I quickly understand mainframe fundamentals without getting lost in the weeds? I relate mainframe concepts to mainstream technologies you already know, giving you the working knowledge you need without requiring you to become a deep specialist.

Who This Book Is For

While I wrote this book for decision-makers - CIOs, IT executives, enterprise architects, and technology directors - I have intentionally made it accessible to anyone who needs to understand mainframe strategy: CFOs evaluating IT investments, architects and technical specialists modernising legacy systems, DevOps leaders, security officers, and consultants advising clients.

You don't need deep mainframe experience to use this book. In fact, if you're coming fresh to the topic, you might find it easier to cut through the mythology that's built up over decades.

What makes this different? It is vendor-neutral. I am not selling you IBM tools or anyone else's products. My aim is to give you the information you need to make your own decisions. It's business-focused, not just a technical manual. And it's as current as possible, covering AI, containers, cloud integration, and where this technology is actually heading.

In Closing

The mainframe question isn't whether the technology has a future. It does. The question is: what role, if any, should it play in yours?

The technology isn't what's holding you back. Uncertainty is.

This book removes that uncertainty.

Now it's your turn to decide.

Niek de Greef
Lead Architect Enterprise Systems
30+ years in mainframe architecture

Table of contents

Table of figures

Chapter 1 Introduction

Does this scenario sound familiar? In 2022, a large European bank faced a critical decision: their mainframe platform, running core banking systems for 15 million customers, was labelled 'legacy' by consultants who recommended a €100M+ migration to the cloud. The CIO asked a simple question: 'But does it actually need replacing?'

No one could answer definitively.

Welcome to the world of IBM mainframes, these robust computing systems that have been the backbone of global enterprise computing for decades, yet remain shrouded in mystery for many technology professionals.

This book aims to demystify mainframe technology, presenting it in accessible terms for readers with a basic understanding of computing concepts.

Mainframe computing is neither inherently more complex nor simpler than other computing environments. It is simply different. Like any specialized technology, it has its own terminology, architecture, and approach to solving business problems.

While technical descriptions are necessary to explain certain fundamental concepts, I have worked to present them in straightforward language. When deeper technical explorations are required, they are marked, and you can skip these sections without losing the broader narrative.

The book explores both architecture and business implications of mainframe systems. IBM mainframes represent significant capital investments that organizations carefully evaluate and maintain over extended periods. Understanding the financial considerations, operational costs, and commercial value proposition of these systems is equally essential as mastering their technical capabilities. This balanced perspective will help you appreciate why mainframes continue to serve as mission-critical infrastructure for many of the world's largest enterprises.

The title "Don't Be Afraid of the Mainframe" reflects my primary mission: to help you feel comfortable and confident with IBM mainframe systems. In my years of experience, I've observed how we "mainframers" sometimes inadvertently intimidate newcomers with specialized jargon and complex terminology.

I hope you enjoy the book, and I welcome your feedback. For more details, visit seneqa.nl.

Niek

Chapter 2 How to navigate this book

This book is designed to cater to diverse reading approaches, tailored to your interests and background. Here's a quick overview of the chapters, followed by a guided tour to help you navigate this book effectively.

Chapter overview

Chapter 3: The mainframe defined
This section introduces the fundamental concept of mainframes, establishing the foundation for all subsequent discussions.

Chapter 4: Mainframe hardware
Explores the physical components that make mainframes unique, from their robust server architecture to specialized hardware components that deliver enterprise-grade performance.

Chapter 5: Mainframe Operating Systems
Provides a comprehensive overview of both legacy and current operating systems available for mainframe environments, tracing their evolutionary development.

Chapter 6: z/OS – the mainframe flagship operating system
Introduces IBM's premier mainframe operating system—the foundation for subsequent chapters exploring middleware, applications, and development practices.

Chapter 7: Middleware for z/OS
Examines the critical intermediary software layer, including application servers, database management systems, and integration tools that bridge applications with the z/OS infrastructure.

Chapter 8: Programming languages for z/OS
Surveys the diverse programming languages supported on z/OS, from traditional COBOL and PL/I to modern languages that extend the platform's capabilities.

Chapter 9: Integration technologies

Explores technologies that enable seamless communication between mainframe applications and distributed systems across the broader IT landscape.

Chapter 10: Linux for the mainframe

Explores the versatility of running Linux and containerized workloads alongside traditional mainframe applications, creating hybrid operational models.

Chapter 11: Application development for z/OS

Bridges traditional mainframe development with contemporary methodologies, including DevOps, agile practices, and automated testing frameworks.

Chapter 12: Security

Delves into z/OS security concepts, frameworks, and best practices for protecting mission-critical applications in a multi-tenant environment.

Chapter 13: System management

Examines tools and practices for efficiently managing and optimizing z/OS environments to ensure maximum availability and performance.

Chapter 14: Modern application architectures

Provides guidance on implementing contemporary architectural patterns within the z/OS environment, striking a balance between innovation and enterprise requirements.

Chapter 15: Understanding mainframe cost

Essential reading for those with financial responsibilities or interests. This chapter breaks down the total cost of ownership and the long-term financial implications of mainframe systems. Technical readers may choose to revisit this later.

Chapter 16: Mainframes in the Cloud Era

Analyzes how cloud computing paradigms influence mainframe evolution and deployment strategies in contemporary IT environments with hybrid architectures.

Chapter 17: Transformation strategies
Provides pragmatic approaches for transforming legacy mainframe applications into future-ready systems, without compromising reliability or business continuity.

Chapter 18: The future of mainframe computing
Synthesizes key insights and examines emerging trends shaping the continued evolution of mainframe technology.

Reading guide per role

To help you navigate the book efficiently, Figure 1 provides a reading guide tailored to different roles.

Chapters 3 and 4 give an overview of what a mainframe is at a minimum technical level. Chapter 18 summarizes the key insights and examines future trends. These chapters are recommended for all readers.

If you're a **CFO**, **IT Executive,** or **Business Leader**, you might start with the Executive Summary, thumb through Chapters 3 and 4, and jump to Chapter 15 (Costs), optionally Chapter 17 (Transformation), and read Chapter 18 (The future).

If you are an **Enterprise Architect**, apart from the Executive Summary, Chapter 3, 4, and 18, read Chapters 9 (Integration), 10 (Linux), 11 (Application Development), 12 (Security and Compliance), 14 (Architecture), and 17 (Transformation). Chapter 16 (Mainframes and Cloud) may also be relevant to you.

As a **Technical Leader or IT Professional,** you can then review all the chapters, follow the book's flow, and explore those that align with your interests and needs. While each chapter builds on the concepts introduced earlier, they are also designed to stand alone, allowing you to focus on the topics most relevant to you.

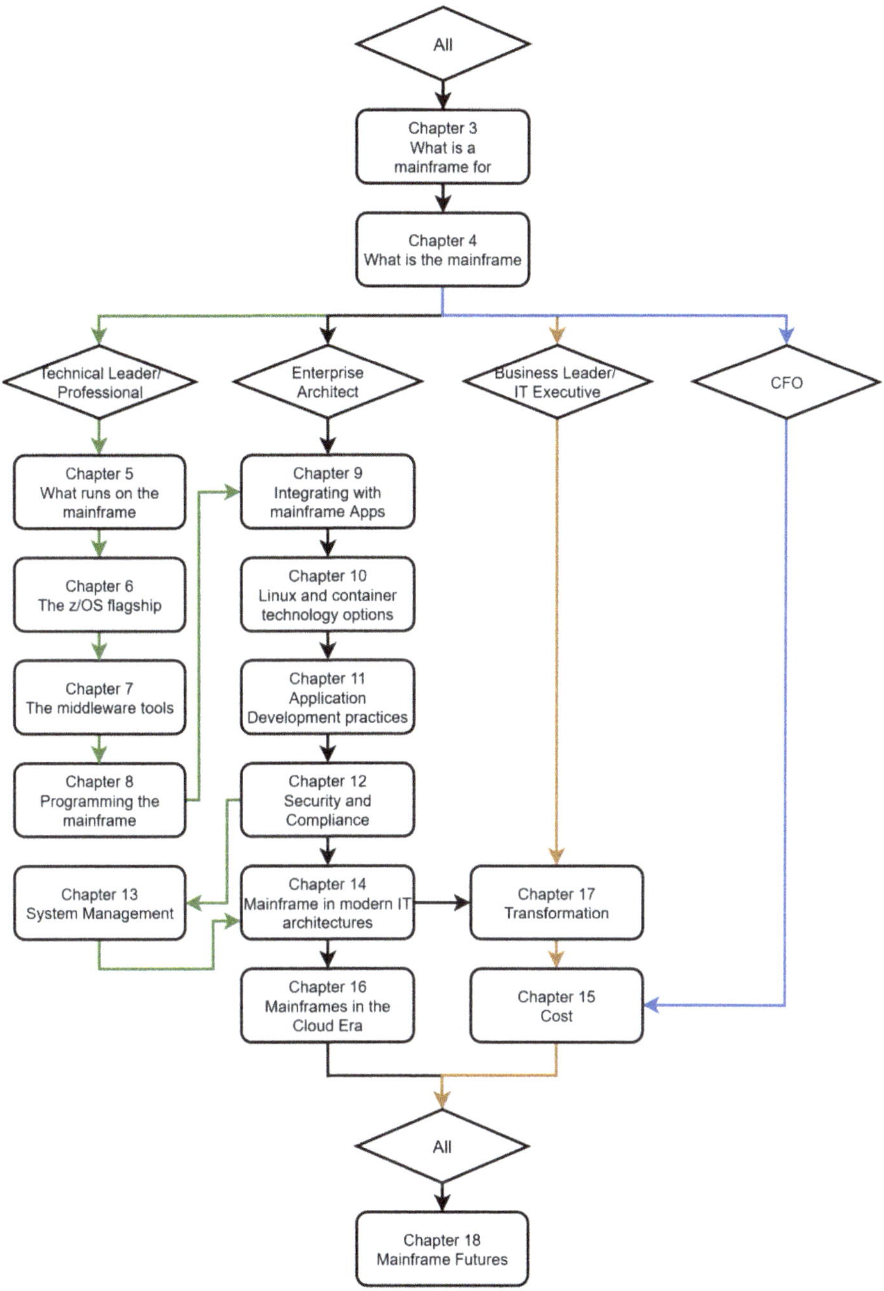

Figure 1 Reading guide by role

Chapter 3 The mainframe defined

To begin, let's define what a mainframe is. Following this definition, we will provide a brief historical overview of mainframes.

The mainframe: a definition

A mainframe is a large, central computer designed to run multiple computing tasks simultaneously in a stable and secure manner.

In this definition, I use the term "computer" to refer to all the hardware and software components necessary to run meaningful application software.

Several key aspects are specifically relevant in defining a mainframe.

Central. The mainframe's design goal is to provide a centralized function for many computing tasks. The mainframe shares computing resources, hardware, and software between applications. The other way around is that many applications use the same mainframe computer.

Many tasks at the same time. From the ground up, the mainframe operating system is designed to run many technical tasks and applications very efficiently.

Secure. Because many applications run on the same computing platform, the mainframe's operating system has sophisticated facilities to ensure that applications can not interfere with each other.

A very brief history

Mainframes date back to a time when computing equipment was costly, and a single central solution was the only way to run computing tasks efficiently.

The early users of the mainframe were primarily large organizations, including banks, insurance companies, government institutions, retailers, and numerous smaller organizations. These organizations have often utilized the mainframe since the 1960s or 1970s, and applications developed during that time are still in use today.

COBOL and PL/I are typical programming languages used to develop business applications for mainframes, although Java has also gained significant popularity, also on mainframes.

The mainframe platform supports an extensive ecosystem of cutting-edge technologies beyond traditional workloads. Organizations can use enterprise-grade application servers, sophisticated integration frameworks, advanced data analytics platforms, and modern artificial intelligence solutions, all optimized for the mainframe environment. The platform's specialized hardware accelerators and software optimizations provide exceptional performance for computationally intensive workloads, including AI for large language models and inferencing. This convergence of established reliability with emerging technologies allows businesses to consolidate diverse workloads on a single platform while maintaining the security, availability, and transactional integrity that mainframes are renowned for delivering.

Mainframes are recognized for their unmatched ability to swiftly, reliably, and securely process and manage vast amounts of data. Their robustness ensures uninterrupted operation for critical applications, making them indispensable for industries such as banking and insurance. With seamless scalability, mainframes can handle growing workloads without compromising performance, providing a strong sense of security for large enterprises. They dominate in high-speed transaction processing, efficiently supporting thousands of applications and users simultaneously. Overall, mainframes are very good at managing large-scale data operations securely and efficiently, making them a cornerstone of many large enterprises.

Many companies have built mainframe computers in the past 70 years. Examples are ICL, Bull, Sperry, Tandem, Siemens, Unisys, and NEC. However, IBM has been by far the most successful mainframe manufacturer, and IBM mainframes have become synonymous with the term 'mainframe.' In this book, I will focus solely on the IBM mainframe, also called IBM Z.

Chapter 4 Mainframe hardware

In this chapter, I will discuss the main hardware concepts of IBM mainframes. I will not go into the tiniest detail, but this will be somewhat technical. I will compare the mainframe technology with more mainstream x86, Windows, and Unix technology to facilitate understanding. You will see there is often just a difference in terminology.

The box, a big box

The mainframe has a long history. Some hardware terminology dates back to the early days of computing and differs from today's usual usage. To understand mainframes, we need to discuss some jargon.

A box full of CPU and memory

A mainframe is a sizable, refrigerator-sized box with computing capacity. The box houses the computing units, the CPUs. These are not Intel x86 CPUs like on your Windows PC. Instead, a mainframe uses CPUs built following the processor architecture designed by IBM, called IBM z/Architecture.

In your PC, the various components, such as the CPU, memory, and other chips, are soldered onto a motherboard. Like your PC, you find a motherboard in the big mainframe box. The mainframe motherboard is called a drawer. The drawer is bigger than your PC's motherboard because it carries more components.

The mainframe's CPU and memory chips are manufactured together with more components in the drawer. A drawer can have several CPU chips. The z14 model, which I use as an example throughout the following sections, has six CPU chips per drawer.

Each CPU chip in the drawer has many processor cores, which are the actual CPUs. The number of processor cores varies per mainframe model. In the z14 mainframe model, there are 10 cores on a chip.

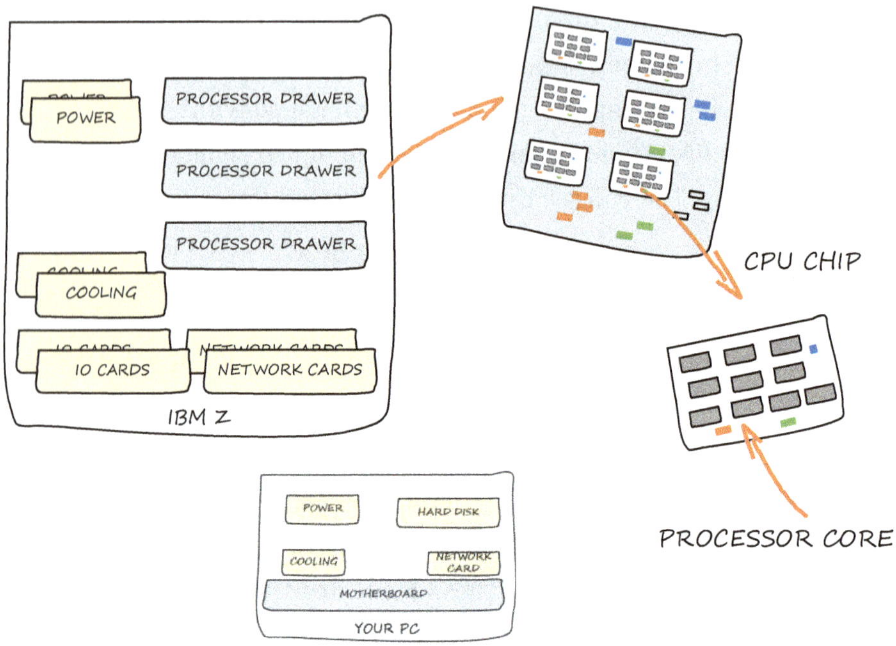

Figure 2 What's in a mainframe server

Finally, you can have multiple drawers in a mainframe box. A z14 mainframe model can have four drawers. All of this is illustrated in Figure 2.

Now, let's count. You can have up to 4 drawers, each with up to 6 CPU chips, each chip with 10 cores. This totals up to 240 processor cores in a mainframe box – the z14 model, to be precise. The mainframe uses a number of these 240 cores for internal processing. As a user, you can utilize up to 170 processor cores in a single mainframe box.

You also need memory. Each drawer on the z14 mainframe supports up to 8 TB of memory, for a total of 32 TB in your z14 mainframe.

A lot of computing power.

I am currently using the IBM z14 mainframe as an example. The latest model at the time of writing is the IBM z17, which features up to 4 processor drawers. Each drawer contains 8 processor chips, each housing 8 cores, delivering impressive computing power. The z17 supports a maximum of 64 terabytes (TB) of memory. That is a capacity equivalent to storing roughly 12 million high-quality digital photos or about 12,000 full-length high-definition movies.

What else is in the box?

In addition to the central computing elements, CPU, and memory, the mainframe server contains almost everything else needed: power supplies, network cards, cooling devices, I/O cards, and more.

Figure 3 IBM z14 mainframe server machine opened up

To ensure that the mainframe can continue running when one of these components fails, all components are redundantly configured in the mainframe. In other words, for each component type, there is at least one spare part in a mainframe.

In the picture of Figure 4, you can see the following components in a real mainframe server:

- Processor drawers – as we saw, the motherboard of the mainframe. Depending on the number of CPUs you have ordered, a machine can have multiple processor drawers.
- PCIe Input Output drawers in which cards are configured for networking equipment, IO interfaces (disk, tape, server-to-server connections), and additional facilities such as encryption and compression. PCIe is a standard for computer interfaces.
- Cooling components regulate the server's temperature. A mainframe box can be water-cooled or air-cooled.
- Power supplies provide power for the machine's components.

It looks much like a regular computer, just a little bigger.

In Figure 4, you also see two laptops. As we will see later, the big box needs to be configured. The two laptops are so-called support elements. You can configure the hardware and monitor its state with these support elements.

Figure 4 The mainframe server's main elements

Peripherals and other quirks

Hard disks

A mainframe server does not have hard disks; similarly, larger x86 servers do not always have hard disks either. However, laptops and PCs always have a hard disk or, nowadays, a solid-state drive (SSD) to store data. The data for the mainframe is stored externally to the mainframe box in separate equipment called storage controllers or storage (sub)systems. The term 'disk' is still used often, but there are no spinning disks anymore; SSDs are now the standard.

A special high-speed network connects a mainframe to its storage. A mainframe runs many business applications and needs much more disk storage than our laptops. Normal storage amounts easily exceed 1000 TB.

Fun quirky thing: on the mainframe, disk storage is often called DASD, an old abbreviation for Direct Access Storage Device. The term has stuck around.

To confuse you further, when mainframers refer to "storage," they may mean memory, the RAM in the box. So be careful with the term storage and clarify what it means when used.

Tape

Many organizations still use tapes to back up and archive data. Tape units are separate hardware systems, often including a "library" or "tape-robot" to register and store the many physical tape cartridges.

Storage network

A special fiber-optic network connects the mainframe servers with the storage hardware. The mainframes use a proprietary SAN (Storage Area Network) protocol called FICON for this connection. Special FICON switches connect mainframe servers to disk and tape systems in such a network.

Printers

Some organizations still have printers connected to their mainframes, but this is less common now. Online applications have replaced most printing facilities, removing the need for print work. Where printing is still needed, it is often done in dedicated centralized printing facilities or outsourced to external firms specializing in printing and distributing paper output.

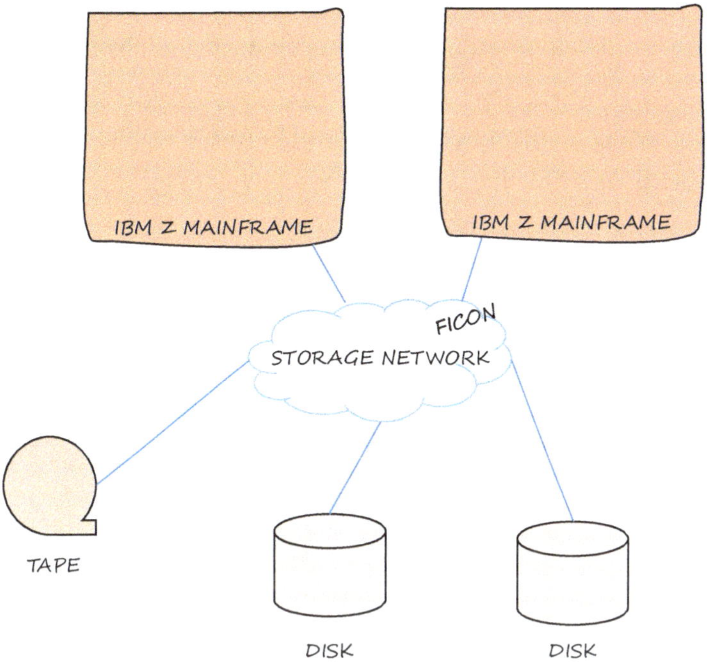

Figure 5 Mainframes and storage devices in a SAN

Big hardware, but partitioned into smaller parts

In the section 'A box full of CPU and memory', we saw that the mainframe server could have a huge computing capacity. With a mainframe, you run all your development, test, acceptance, and production environments on this large box. To do this efficiently, you must create logical environments for that big server. Mainframe technology provides many facilities to achieve this.

One of the main tools for splitting hardware into logical and physical parts is PR/SM (pronounced "prism"). This tool partitions the mainframe into smaller virtual servers, called logical partitions (LPARs). In an LPAR, you can run your test or production system.

A common way to split mainframe computing capacity is to assign separate LPARs to Development, Testing, Acceptance, and Production work.

In larger computing environments, separate LPARs are usually used for different applications or business units. The way you divide the mainframe logically is entirely up to you.

A bank may have separate LPARs for its wholesale and retail businesses, and other organizations may have separate LPARs for their business analytics and logistics applications.

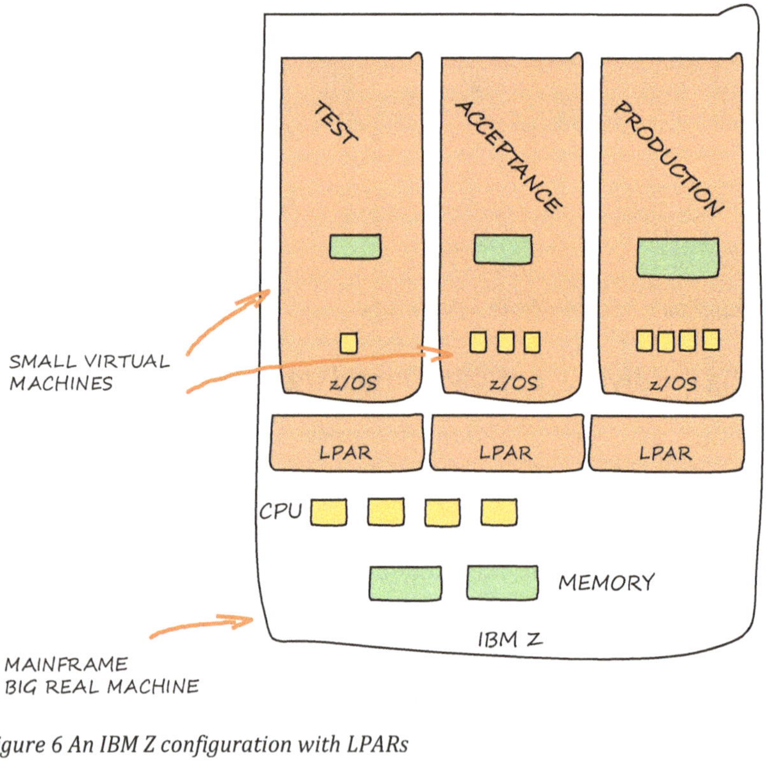

Figure 6 An IBM Z configuration with LPARs

Specialty engines

A mainframe has many CPUs. The CPUs can be configured in different modes: a general-purpose mode and several specialty modes.

General-purpose CPUs versus specialty engines

The regular use of a CPU is referred to as a *general-purpose CPU*. Alternatively, a CPU can be configured as a so-called *specialty engine*. This is a special sort of setup that only an IBM engineer can arrange. Typically, this is agreed upon when configuring and purchasing mainframe hardware in collaboration with IBM.

As the name suggests, a general-purpose CPU can be used for a wide range of tasks. However, it is used only for traditional workload types, such as applications written in COBOL and PL/I.

When a CPU is configured as a specialty engine, the CPU can *only* be used for a special function. So, a specialty engine is not special because it is designed for a particular function. Instead, it is a regular CPU that is configured to perform only a specific function.

The purpose of specialty engines is to make running particular functions on the mainframe cheaper. For traditional workloads that run on general-purpose CPUs, you pay your regular software bill based on MSUs. I will talk about this in the chapter "Understanding mainframe cost".

The key point here is that functions that run on a specialty engine are not accounted for in the MSU numbers and, therefore, are not used to calculate the software bill for z/OS software. This makes it a lot cheaper to run particular workloads on specialty engines.

It is up to your software vendor to decide if their software runs on a specialty engine. IBM has enabled certain z/OS, Db2, and Java functions for specialty engines, and other vendors have done so similarly for selected mainframe software components.

It is also important to realize that even though the general-purpose and specialty engines are the same hardware, the price of a specialty engine is significantly lower than that of a general-purpose CPU.

Types of specialty engines

The most important types of specialty engines for mainframe users are the so-called zIIP and IFL engines. I will spare you the meaning of these abbreviations—nobody uses these.

A *zIIP* is a specialty engine that can only be used on the z/OS operating system. The special functions you can run on a zIIP are all Java programs, certain Db2 functions, selected other functions, and zCX Containers (more on that in section z/OS Container Extensions). Many mainframe software vendors enable their software for zIIPs and offer special conditions for these products to lower the cost of deploying their tools.

An *IFL* is another specialty engine; this CPU can only be used for Linux work on the mainframe. IFLs can not be used for z/OS. You use IFLs in LPARs running the Linux operating system. I will discuss Linux on the mainframe in a dedicated chapter 'Linux for the mainframe'.

The other types of specialty engines enable CPUs in the mainframe for special technical computing processes, which are needed to support "real" business workloads. The CPU usage is, therefore, also not accounted for in the software bill. These processor types are the following:

- The *Integrated Coupling Facility (ICF)* CPU is used with a Coupling Facility. A Coupling Facility is a special LPAR that provides unique operating system functions for a parallel sysplex, the clustering function in z/OS. We will discuss the sysplex and Coupling Facility concepts in the 'Parallel Sysplex' section.
- The *System Assistance Processor (SAP)* specialty engine runs I/O operations independently from your central CPUs in a mainframe component called the IO Subsystem. This CPU type transports data

between memory and storage. This makes I/O processing independent of central computing in a mainframe, increasing the speed and capacity of the mainframe. Also, this ensures that IO processing does not affect your software bill.

AI Accelerators for IBM Z

A recent development is IBM's evolution of the Telum and Spyre. These processors are designed specifically to meet the demands of enterprise workloads in the era of artificial intelligence and real-time analytics.

The Telum processor is built onto the Z processor chip. Telum thus embeds AI inference into the mainframe's central processor, enabling you to run inference operations directly within transaction processing flows without requiring callouts to external systems. This capability promises to be valuable for applications such as fraud detection in financial transactions, where milliseconds can make a critical difference.

The Spyre AI accelerator is the latest development, bringing AI learning capabilities to the mainframe. A Spyre is delivered as a PCIe or plug-in card and is optimized for AI matrix operations, with direct data transfer between compute engines to improve energy efficiency. Spyre is very similar to the GPU processors for AI in other computer architectures. Spyre enables more intensive and complex AI workloads and models for inferencing and generative and agentic AI.

Chapter 5 Mainframe Operating Systems

In the previous chapter, I provided an overview of the most essential mainframe hardware components. This chapter summarizes what operating systems can run on this hardware.

First, what is an operating system? A computer's operating system is the essential software between the hardware and the applications. Windows and Linux are operating systems for mainstream computers, and similar software is used on mainframes.

z/OS

IBM often calls z/OS its flagship mainframe operating system. The roots of z/OS go back to 1964. The operating system OS/360 was designed for the System/360 computer, the predecessor of IBM's modern mainframe computers.

In the early 70s, IBM developed the successor to OS/360. It was named MVS, which stands for Multiple Virtual Storage. MVS evolved further into MVX/XA, MVS/ESA, and OS/390, and today's z/OS operating system. The name changes may suggest fundamentally different systems, but these are only marketing-driven name changes for MVS. The technology base remains the same, though it has evolved significantly.

z/VM, the mother of all hypervisors

z/VM is another operating system for the mainframe with a lot of history. VM stands for Virtual Machine. z/VM, or VM as it was initially called, was designed as an alternative operating system for running business applications on the mainframe. The z/VM operating system included unique technology that allowed users to virtualize hardware and split it into small parts: virtual machines. Nowadays, tools like VMWare, KVM, Xen, Hyper-V, and others provide the same concept for x86 and other hardware. However, the hypervisor technology in z/VM was developed in the 1960s and was far ahead of its time. z/VM can be considered the mother of all hypervisors.

Today, z/VM remains a key hypervisor for IBM mainframes, mainly for Linux on the mainframe, although its role as a full operating system for business applications has diminished. With the advent of the KVM hypervisor on the mainframe, KVM is increasingly being adopted alongside and in some cases, gradually replacing z/VM for managing Linux virtual servers. One significant advantage of KVM, and more recently of KubeVirt and OpenShift virtualization running on top of it, is that it is an open-source solution with a broader user base and community support than the more specialized z/VM. KVM integrates more seamlessly with modern virtualization and container orchestration platforms such as Kubernetes and OpenShift, enabling hybrid environments that combine virtual machines and container workloads more efficiently.

This shift reflects a broader industry trend toward open, flexible, and cloud-native infrastructure management. KVM and KubeVirt provide a more familiar, extensible ecosystem for Linux-savvy administrators and developers while still leveraging the scalability and reliability of mainframe hardware. I will discuss Linux in more depth in the chapter "Linux for the Mainframe."

z/VSE

The z/VSE operating system is z/OS's smaller sibling, developed by IBM alongside MVS for mid-sized customers like payroll providers and firms in manufacturing and transportation. It has fewer scalability options, and few middleware tools are available on z/VSE. Many z/VSE users have migrated to z/OS over the past decades, but there are still many users of the z/VSE operating system. IBM transferred the development and distribution of z/VSE to the U.S. company 21st Century Software (21CS).

VSE is now rebranded to VSE^{n} and 21CS continues to develop and maintain the platform.

z/TPF

The z/TPF (Transaction Processing Facility) operating system was developed as a specialized real-time system. Organizations that need to quickly process large volumes of small transactions, such as credit card companies, airline and hotel reservation systems, and banks, have deployed this specialized mainframe operating system.

Linux on IBM Z

IBM ported Linux to its mainframe architecture and announced its first release in 2000. Since then, many other commercial and open-source software products have been made available on Linux on IBM Z.

Configurations for Linux on the mainframe are typically virtualized using z/VM, the mainframe hypervisor we previously discussed, or KVM, an open-source hypervisor. With z/VM and KVM, you can create and manage many Linux virtual servers on the mainframe. Additionally, you can run Linux containers on the mainframe. I will explore this topic further in the chapter on Linux for the mainframe.

What's next in this book

In the remainder of the book, I will focus on the two most important mainframe operating systems today. z/OS is the most widely used operating system on mainframes. I will discuss z/OS in greater detail in the next chapter.

Linux is the second-most-popular operating system on mainframes. Linux has gained popularity over the past decade. I will discuss Linux in Chapter 'Linux for the mainframe' and show what Linux configurations on the mainframe typically look like.

Chapter 6 z/OS – the mainframe flagship operating system

This chapter introduces the main z/OS concepts and terminology to help you understand them. I will also explain how z/OS peculiarities relate to more commonly known concepts in Unix and Windows.

I will look at z/OS from the traditional MVS perspective and the more relatable Unix perspective. The traditional MVS perspective dates back to the 1960s and differs most from what we know of Windows and Unix. The Unix part is an extension IBM developed for z/OS in the 1990s that runs Unix applications, much like other Unix flavors.

Next, I will discuss the unique clustering facility that z/OS offers, named Parallel Sysplex.

Finally, I will examine the green-screen user interface often associated with the mainframe. I will discuss where green-screen tools are still necessary, and where not, and describe modern z/OS tools with more sophisticated graphical user interfaces.

The MVS part of z/OS

The MVS side of z/OS is the traditional 'old-school' mainframe side rooted in the 1960s. These MVS functions stem from an era when punch cards contained the program code. You fed a stack of punch cards into a punch card reader connected to the computer to get something done. In the MVS part of z/OS, these old features remain. Today, many look a bit awkward.

The basic operation of the MVS part with batch and JCL

First, I will look at the basic operation of a batch process in z/OS. Batch processing is the style of computing with which you prepare input data to be processed, start the computing process, wait a while, and receive the output data as a result. There is no interactivity in a batch process.

The batch process is a core concept in the MVS part of z/OS. In essence, today's batch processing still works the same way as it was designed in the 1960s. To run a program on z/OS, you need a way to instruct z/OS on what to do. You do this by writing a script. The language used for this z/OS script is called JCL – Job Control Language.

With the JCL script, you tell the computer which program to run, specify the input for that program, and where to write the output. The JCL code looks like this:

```
//MYTSTJOB JOB (ACT123,'DEPT56'),'JOHN SMITH',
//              CLASS=A,
//              MSGCLASS=X,
//              MSGLEVEL=(1,1),
//              NOTIFY=&SYSUID,
//              REGION=0M
//RUNPROG   EXEC PGM=PROGRAM1
//INPUT     DD DISP=SHR,DSN=MY.INPUT.DATA
//OUTPUT    DD DISP=NEW,MY.OUTPUT.DATA
```

This code looks terrible, of course, despite its simplicity. The JCL language employs odd forward slashes, fixed key field positions, etc. Many of these characters exist because the JCL language was designed for punch cards. Punch cards could hold a maximum of 80 characters per line, and each line also required specific positions to control the operation of the punch card reader. Everything had to be coded in uppercase to simplify things for the punch card reader. While JCL is easily readable by a punch card reader device, it is an ugly phenomenon from an aesthetic and ergonomic standpoint. Punch cards have vanished, yet the JCL language persists.

Returning to the JCL snippet above, the first statement is the JOB statement. The term 'job' is mainframe terminology for a computing process. The JOB statement names the job (MYTSTJOB) and sets operational parameters. Next, with the EXEC statement, you tell the computer to run PROGRAM1 with this script. You use the file referenced by the INPUT label as input, and the file referenced by the label OUTPUT as the output file. If you feed this into the mainframe running z/OS, it will try to execute it as such. Figure 7 illustrates this process.

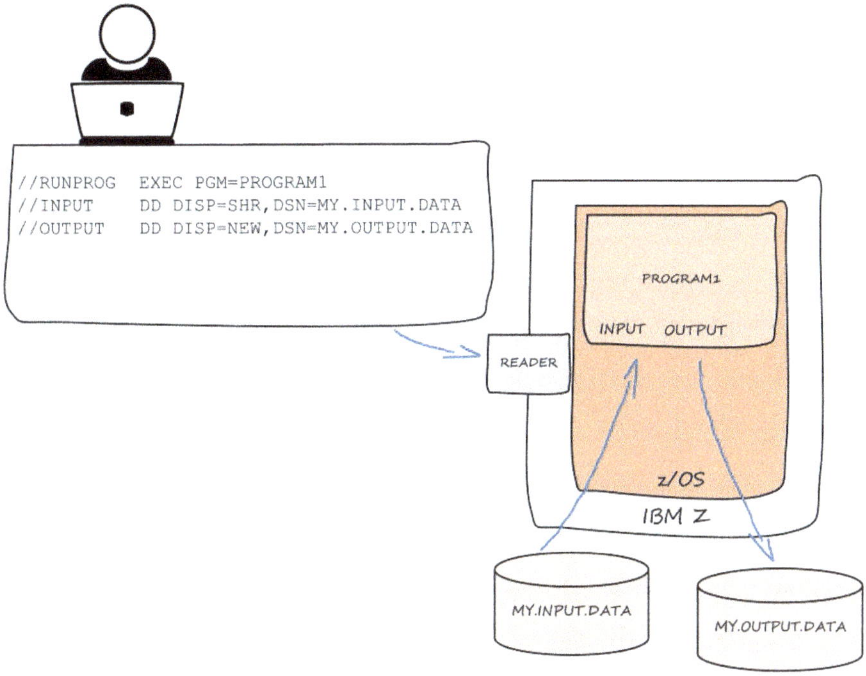

Figure 7 JCL describes the work to be done

In the old days, the programmer punched JCL on paper punch cards with a special punch card machine, creating one card for every JCL line. She then carried the stack of cards to the data center building and inserted them into a punch card reader attached to the mainframe. The punch card reader read the stack of cards and executed the program.

Card reader devices no longer exist. Instead, a software component in z/OS replaces them. This software function is called the internal reader.

The user can start his program by typing a "Submit" command with the JCL as a parameter or selecting the Submit option in the user interface of a modern IDE, as illustrated in Figure 8.

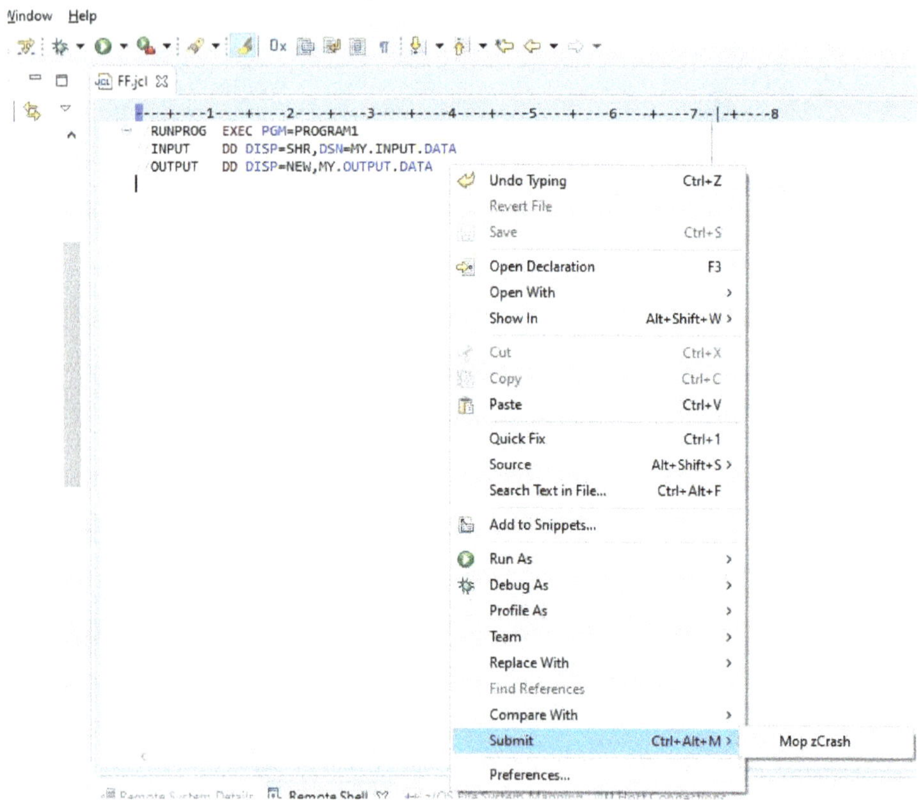

Figure 8 Submit JCL from a modern IDE

Now, the internal reader component of z/OS reads the JCL, locates the program and its required files, and starts the program's execution.

Address Spaces are processes

A dedicated computer process executes a program on z/OS. In Unix and Windows, the concept of execution is simply called a *process*. However, in the MVS part of z/OS, this concept is called an *Address Space*. You can imagine that many tasks are running simultaneously for numerous users. All these tasks operate in Address Spaces on z/OS. If there were a Task Manager on z/OS like the one in Windows, you would see Address Spaces listed there. In fact, there is an equivalent to a Task Manager in z/OS, as we will see later in this book.

Although the name "Address Space" suggests it is related to memory, it is the same concept as a *process* in Windows and Unix.

Side note: Virtual storage is memory

The Address Space provides the program with the memory it needs to execute. On z/OS, this memory is called virtual storage.

The odd thing I mentioned before is that Mainframers often refer to memory as *storage* or *virtual storage*. They could do this without getting confused by disk storage, since that was called DASD, which stands for Direct Access Storage Device.

Datasets, files, and catalogs

In the MVS part of z/OS, data is persisted in file structures called *datasets*. Datasets are just like files as you know them, but with some quirks, which I will discuss in the next section.

These MVS datasets are registered in *catalogs*. Catalogs administer all datasets and register where each dataset is stored on disk. I will discuss catalogs later in this chapter.

Datasets are record-oriented and can have different structures

On IBM mainframes, datasets are specialized data storage structures that differ from ordinary files in that they are record-oriented. Each dataset's internal structure is defined by its *record format*, which dictates how data is organized. When creating a dataset, you must specify metadata parameters such as:

- The record format, which defines whether records are fixed-length (every record has the same byte size) or variable-length (records can vary in size).
- The dataset size.
- The record length, which defines the number of bytes per record (fixed) or the maximum allowed length (variable).

The dataset type determines its logical organization. You have *sequential datasets* that use a linear layout. You also have *VSAM datasets* (Virtual Storage Access Method), which use a hierarchical structure to support advanced access patterns.

Sequential datasets

Sequential datasets are ordered from the first record to the last. To read or write a sequential dataset, a program starts at the beginning and proceeds to the next record until completion. Processing a sequential file is very much like reading a file in Unix or Windows.

VSAM datasets

VSAM datasets have very specific internal structures. There are five main VSAM data set types, each optimized for specific access patterns.

1. KSDS (Key-Sequenced Data Set): Records are indexed by a unique key. The most commonly used VSAM type today. Used for database implementations such as Db2 for z/OS. I will talk about this type a bit more below.
2. ESDS (Entry-Sequenced Data Set): Records are laid out in arrival order. This is used in middleware components for logs and queues.

3. RRDS (Relative Record Data Set): Records can be directly accessed by position. This is very fast and used for very specific middleware and operating system components.
4. LDS (Linear Data Set): For unstructured byte streams. Used for operating system functions, such as page and swap files.

Understanding the difference between VSAM datasets and sequential files

I will explain a bit more about VSAM datasets here, using VSAM KSDS as an example, and compare that to sequential files.

VSAM (KSDS) datasets have an internal database structure. The records you store in a VSAM file have a key value. You do not usually browse the VSAM dataset sequentially; instead, you read or write a specific record directly using its key value. z/OS looks up or creates the record in the file with that key value. To do this, VSAM keeps indexes of key values and records. The benefit of VSAM files is that they provide high-speed access to the stored records. The principle of sequential and VSAM files is illustrated in Figure 9.

When creating an MVS dataset, you are often asked for details such as disk block size and the number of cylinders or tracks the dataset will occupy. These terms come from older storage technology with rotating disks and were used to optimize access speed and storage. Although modern storage uses solid-state devices and these details are largely obsolete, they still appear in z/OS dataset definitions. Unfortunately, they are not always hidden from users, so you will likely encounter them when working with z/OS. (The rationale for keeping these details is to ensure the mainframe's superb backward compatibility, but this can also become an obstacle to change.)

Modern applications built on z/OS should only use sequential files. The problems VSAM solved for applications in the past can now be solved much more easily in a database management system like Db2. VSAM's primary use remains for special-purpose operating systems and middleware datasets when low-level, high-speed, optimized access to data is required. Its complexity remains under the hood of z/OS and the middleware.

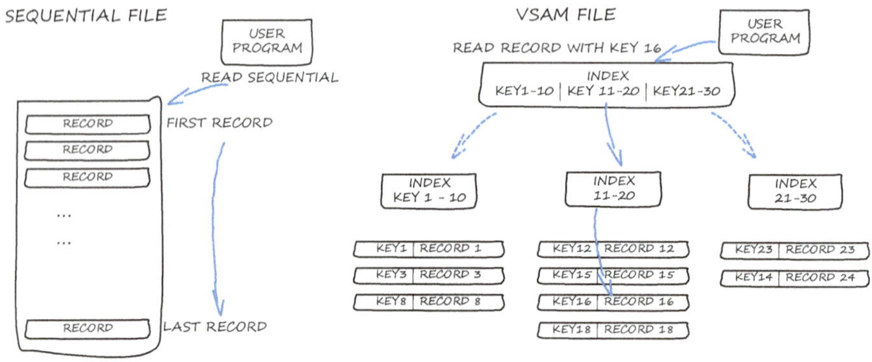

Figure 9 Sequential and VSAM file structures

When you compare a Unix or Windows file to a sequential dataset, you notice that files in Unix and Windows lack the prescribed structure of an MVS dataset. From the user's perspective, a file on Windows and Unix is simply a large string of bytes. The data in these files must be organized internally, often using control characters such as Carriage Return (CR) and Linefeed (LF). See Figure 10. The applications themselves must provide the necessary structure for the files.

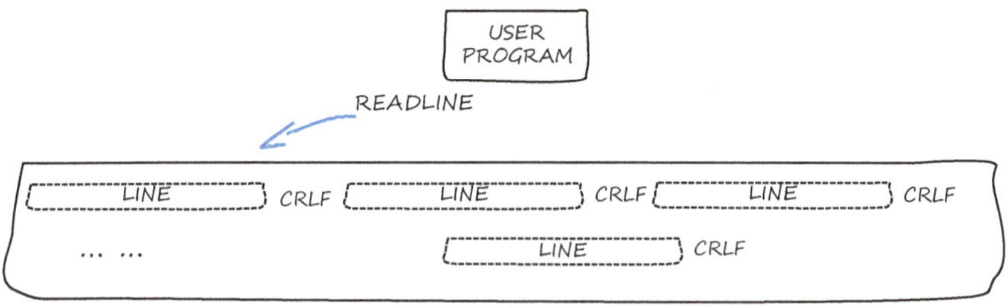

Figure 10 File structure in Unix

The EBCDIC character set

In a computer, each text character in the alphabet, each number character 0 – 9, and other characters are represented by a digital number. The numbering scheme on z/OS is known as EBCDIC, which refers to the EBCDIC character set.

Another character set, ASCII, was used for Unix and Windows, with different digital representations of the characters. Most systems you are familiar with use ASCII. Even more common nowadays is the use of the Unicode character set.

Typically, you may not notice anything unusual about this, and you will likely be unaware of the EBCDIC representation of data. However, if you intend to transfer files between Windows or Unix and z/OS datasets, you'll need to convert the digital representation of characters from ASCII to EBCDIC and vice versa. Generally, file transfer programs can handle this conversion for you as part of the transfer process, but you must instruct them correctly.

Catalogs are like directories

Unix and Windows files are organized in a directory structure, with a file system hierarchy managing the various disks where they can be stored. File systems are defined on hard disks and contain physical files, while the directory structure provides an organized hierarchical structure for those files. The root file system includes the operating system's core files, and additional file systems can be mounted to extend file storage across multiple storage devices.

The Unix and Windows operating systems can find a file if you give it the file name and the directory where it is located.

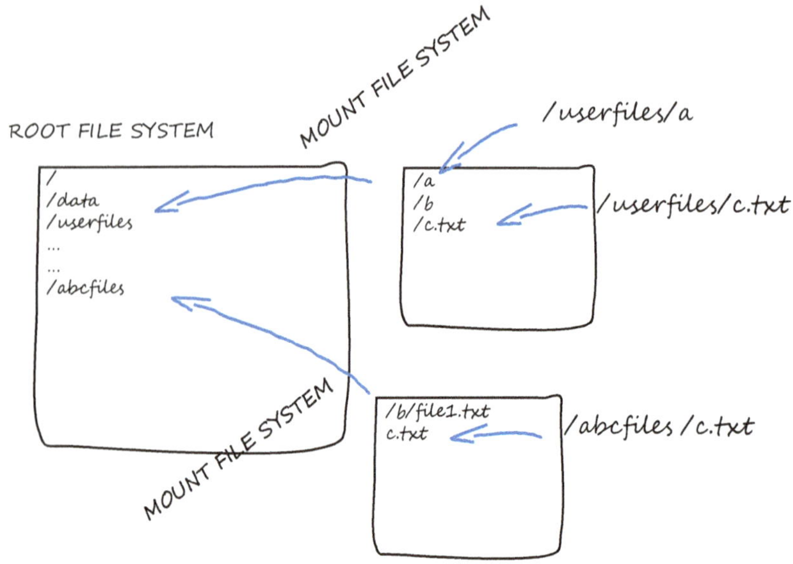

Figure 11 File system and directory structures

In the MVS part of z/OS, the datasets are organized in catalogs. A catalog is an index of dataset names in the z/OS system and the disk volumes on which the datasets are stored. With the catalog mechanism, if the user knows the dataset name, the catalog can tell which disk it is on.

Catalogs are divided into a master catalog and user catalogs. There is one master catalog, but multiple user catalogs may exist. Typically, the master catalog contains only information about system datasets, while user catalogs contain information about datasets for users and applications. The system administrator can determine which datasets are managed within each catalog. When the administrator chooses to manage datasets for application APP2 in a specific user catalog, they add a brief entry in the master catalog to notify z/OS. This entry is known as an ALIAS.

To find a dataset with a specific name, z/OS first looks in the master catalog. z/OS finds it there, or it finds an ALIAS reference. The ALIAS reference tells z/OS to look in the associated user catalog for a dataset with a specific name. When z/OS locates an entry for a dataset, it uses the disk name in the index entry to access the file on disk.

Again, comparing this to Unix, the master catalog functions similarly to the root filesystem: it serves the operating system and middleware datasets. The user catalogs are like mounted file systems for application and user datasets.

However, a catalog is a registration separate from physical storage. In Unix, file registration is done on the filesystems themselves. With a catalog, this is not the case. A catalog is just a dataset, a VSAM dataset to be precise, which can be stored on any disk (I will not bother you with some restrictions that do apply).

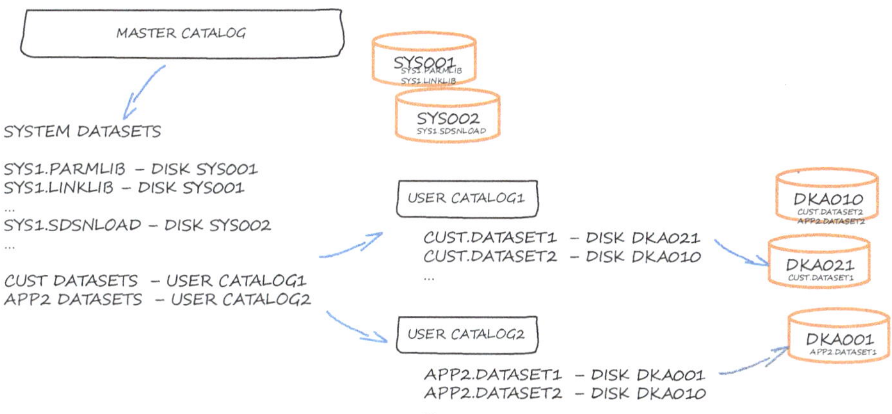

Figure 12 The structure of the master and user catalogs

I will now set aside the MVS peculiarities and turn to the Unix side of z/OS.

The Unix parts of z/OS

In the 1990s, IBM added Unix functionality to z/OS. The first extension was z/OS Unix System Services (z/OS Unix), and recently IBM added z/OS Container Extensions (zCX). I will discuss both in the following sections.

z/OS Unix

The Unix component of z/OS is a runtime environment that plays an integral role in the z/OS operating system. z/OS Unix is fully compliant with Unix (POSIX) standards. It provides an interactive command interface known as a shell in Unix terminology.

IBM developed this part in the 1990s to facilitate porting applications from other platforms to z/OS. Many off-the-shelf and open-source middleware and application packages available on z/OS use z/OS Unix. Examples include IBM's WebSphere Application Server and IBM Integration Bus, the banking product BASE24-eps from ACI, and open-source tools such as PHP and Git.

z/OS Unix has regular files, just like other Unix systems. In the z/OS Unix shell, you can use standard Unix commands such as ls, cd, and more. There is a bash shell, the de facto Unix shell standard, and you can establish a telnet or SSH session with z/OS Unix and perform the same tasks through it as in other Unix environments.

z/OS Container Extensions

Introduced in 2019, z/OS Container Extensions (zCX) enables Linux Docker containers to run natively on z/OS. This innovation bridges the gap between traditional mainframe workloads and modern containerized applications, offering a lightweight, hardware-independent way to deploy Linux applications alongside z/OS.

Linux containers, available on x86 platforms for some time already, provide isolation without the overhead of full virtual machines. Each container runs only the Linux facilities an application needs, allowing dozens of applications to share a single operating system image efficiently. zCX brings this agility to the mainframe, letting you deploy Linux on Z containers using standard Docker commands, with no z/OS expertise required.

What makes zCX particularly even more powerful is its support for OpenShift Container Platform, the enterprise-grade Kubernetes distribution. OpenShift is the de facto standard for container management, offering security, scalability, and integration with cloud-native workflows. With zCX, you can run OpenShift clusters on z/OS, using CRI-O (a lightweight, Kubernetes-optimized container runtime) to manage containers. This means you can:

- Standardize container operations across x86, cloud, and mainframe environments.
- Integrate mainframe applications into hybrid cloud architectures.
- Leverage Kubernetes features like auto-scaling and self-healing, all on the mainframe.

Conceptually, zCX aligns well with z/OS's own architecture. Just as z/OS uses address spaces to isolate applications, Linux containers provide similar isolation on a shared OS kernel. This parallel makes zCX a natural fit for the mainframe, combining its extreme reliability with the flexibility of modern containers.

I will discuss container technology on IBM Z in the chapter Linux on IBM Z.

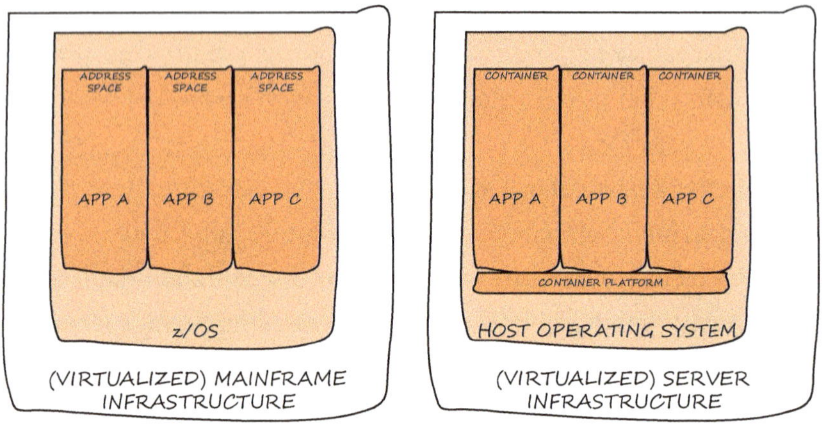

Figure 13 z/OS Address Spaces versus Linux containers

Making Sense of Unix and Linux on IBM Z

You might be wondering: What's the difference between z/OS Unix, z/OS Container Extensions, and Linux for Z? Let's clarify these terms, as they represent distinct but complementary ways to run Unix-like workloads on IBM Z.

- z/OS Unix is an integral part of z/OS itself. It provides a Unix-like environment *within* z/OS, allowing you to run Unix applications natively on the mainframe. However, it is *not* Linux—it's z/OS's own Unix implementation.
- z/OS Container Extensions (zCX) takes this a step further. With zCX, you can run Linux containers on z/OS. These containers use the *Linux flavor* of Unix, not the z/OS Unix flavor. In short: zCX lets you deploy Linux applications in containers, directly within the z/OS environment.
- Linux for Z is a completely separate operating system. It runs in its own LPAR or virtual machine, independent of z/OS. Applications on Linux for Z use the full Linux OS, not z/OS or its Unix environment.

To visualize these relationships, see Figure 14, which illustrates:

- z/OS Unix as part of the z/OS operating system.
- zCX, where Linux Docker containers run as z/OS container processes.
- Linux for Z, operating in its own LPAR, separate from z/OS.

This distinction is crucial: while z/OS Unix and zCX are built into z/OS, Linux for Z is a standalone OS that offers flexibility based on your workload and isolation needs.

Figure 14 The Unix flavors of z/OS and Linux for Z

Parallel Sysplex

One of z/OS's most distinguishing features is the ability to cluster z/OS systems into a Parallel Sysplex. Parallel Sysplex, or Sysplex in short, is a feature of z/OS built in the 1990s that enables extreme scalability and availability.

A cluster of z/OS instances

With Parallel Sysplex, you can configure a cluster of z/OS operating system instances. In such a sysplex, you can combine the computing power of multiple z/OS instances on multiple mainframe servers into a single logical z/OS instance.

When you run your application on a sysplex, it runs across all the sysplex instances. If you need more processing power for your application, you can add CPUs to one or more of the instances or add a new z/OS system to the sysplex.

The sysplex concept makes the z/OS infrastructure extremely scalable; also, a sysplex isolates your applications from software and hardware component failures. If a system or component in a Parallel Sysplex fails, the sysplex software will signal this. z/OS will isolate the failed part while your application continues processing on the surviving instances in the sysplex without interruption.

Special sysplex components: the Coupling Facility

A special component is used for a Parallel Sysplex configuration: the Coupling Facility. This Coupling Facility is a shared-memory and communication vehicle for all the z/OS members in a sysplex.

The z/OS operating system and the middleware can share data in the Coupling Facility. These are types of shared data that all cluster members should know about, since they are used for status information, locking resources accessed concurrently by members, and caching shared data from databases.

A Coupling Facility runs on a dedicated, specialized operating system in its own LPAR. In that sense, it is an appliance.

A sysplex with Coupling Facilities is depicted in Figure 15. There are multiple Coupling Facilities to avoid a single point of failure. The z/OS LPARs in the sysplex connect to the Coupling Facilities. I have not included all the required cross-connections in this picture because that would have made it cluttered.

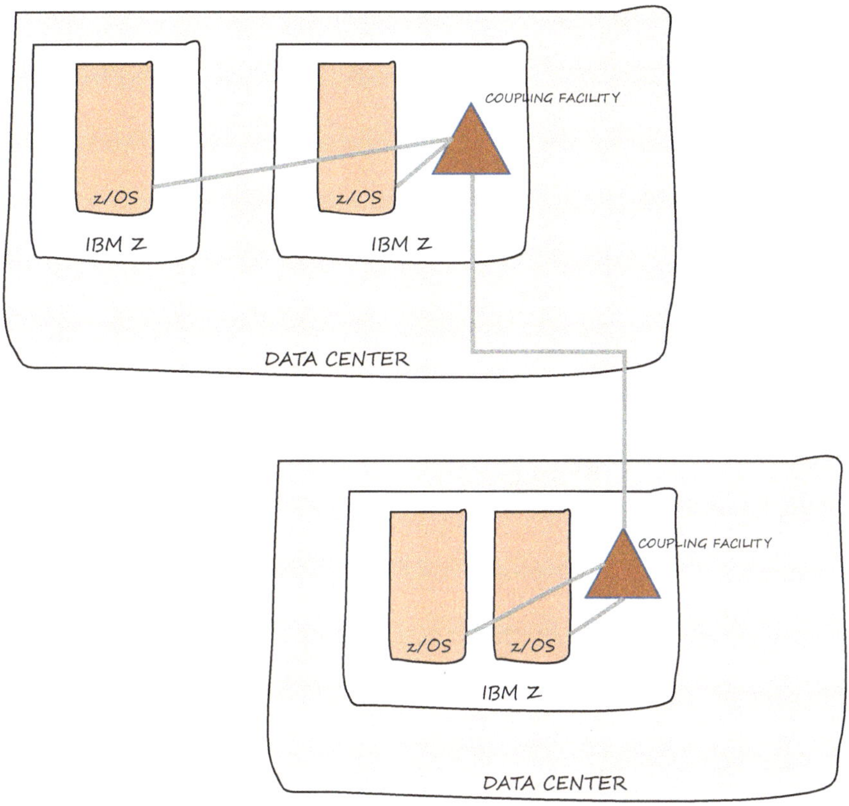

Figure 15 A Parallel Sysplex

Middleware exploits the sysplex functions

Middleware components can use the sysplex features provided by z/OS to create clusters of middleware software.

Db2 can be clustered into so-called Data Sharing Groups. In a Data Sharing Group, you can create a database to process queries on multiple Db2 instances in multiple z/OS instances.

Similarly, WebSphere MQ can be configured within a Queue Sharing Group, CICS within a CICSPlex, IMS within an IMSPlex, and other software, such as WebSphere Application Server, IDMS, and Adabas, can utilize Parallel Sysplex functions to create highly available and scalable clusters.

Figure 16 illustrates this concept. Here, you see a cluster setup of CICS and Db2 in a sysplex. Both CICS and Db2 form a logical middleware instance.

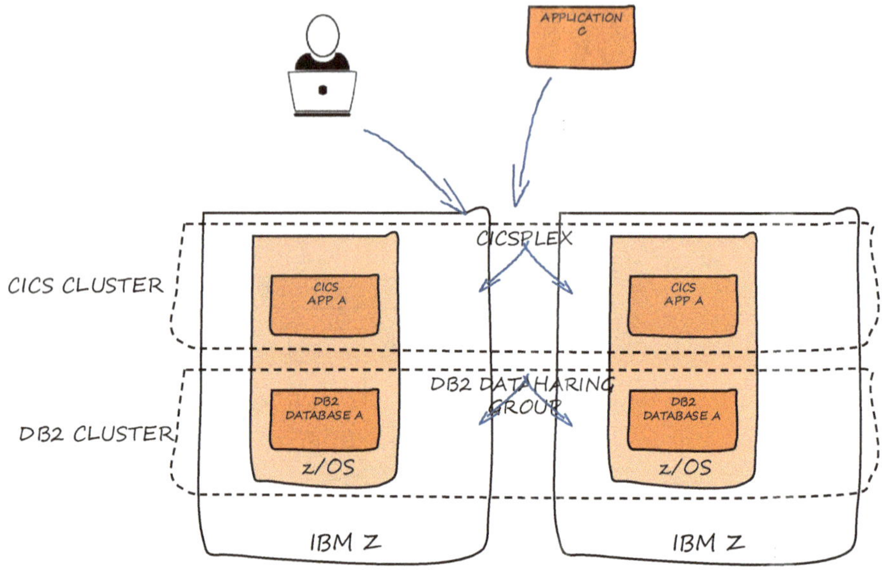

Figure 16 A sysplex cluster with Db2 and CICS

The significant benefit of Parallel Sysplex is its generic capability to build scalable, highly available clusters of middleware solutions.

How is this different from other clustering technologies?

What makes a Parallel Sysplex unique is that it is a clustering facility built into the operating system.

Similar clustering solutions can be achieved on other operating systems, but each middleware component must provide its own clustering features to achieve such a scalable, highly available configuration. This often requires additional components, leading to more complex solutions. And these clusters are not integrated, so they cannot be operated uniformly.

With Parallel Sysplex, clustering is implemented as a central facility within the z/OS operating system.

Extending sysplex with GDPS

An extension of Parallel Sysplex is Geographically Dispersed Parallel Sysplex (GDPS). GDPS provides an additional solution to ensure your data remains available in case of failures. With GDPS, you can ensure that even in the event of a severe hardware failure or a whole data center outage, your data remains available in a secondary data center, with minimal to no disruption to the applications running on z/OS.

In a GDPS configuration, your data is mirrored between storage systems in the two data centers. One site has the primary storage system, and the storage system in the other data center receives a copy of all updates. If the primary storage system or data center fails, GDPS automatically makes the secondary storage device the primary, without disrupting any running applications. This is illustrated in Figure 17. In the event of a failure in one of your data centers, GDPS can even switch all your LPARs in that data center to another data center (or data centers if you have more than two) without disrupting the applications. Thus, GDPS delivers a unique Continuous Availability solution.

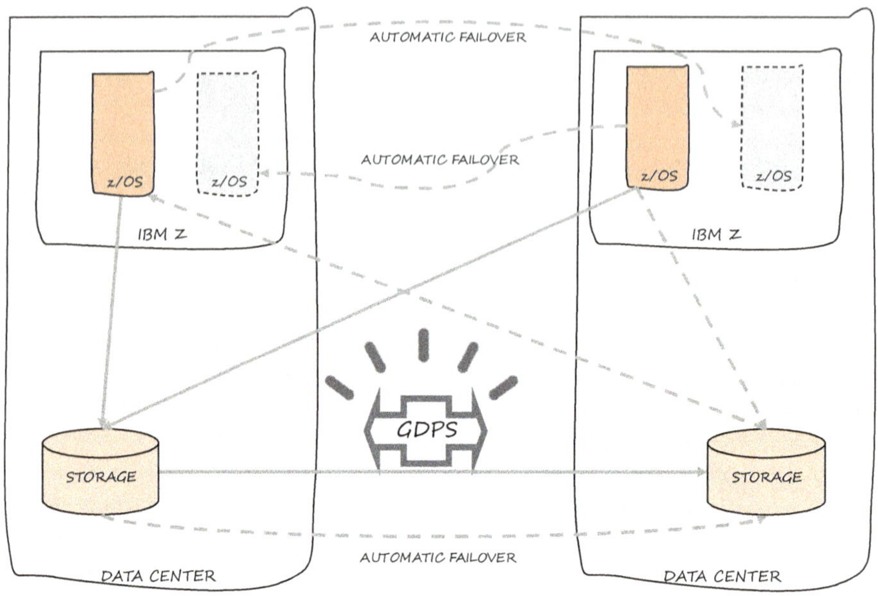

Figure 17 GDPS overview

The interface to z/OS and the green-screen myth

In the previous sections, I have shown you many modern technologies available on z/OS. Still, when you think of the mainframe, you think of a black screen with green characters, which looks cool in The Matrix movie but not so much in real life. Where does this green screen image come from?

In this section, I will briefly discuss the origins of green screens in mainframe technology and show that they have become as common as the DOS prompt or the command prompt in Windows or Linux.

Green screens are for administrators and programmers, not end-users

The green screens on the mainframe are user interfaces. In the early days, programmers created programs on paper behind their desks. They then entered the programs on punch cards or paper tape. These media were then fed into the computers using a special reader device.

In the 1960s, computers with terminal interfaces – screens and keyboards - were built. With these terminals, users could enter programs and data online. The green screens originated in the 1960s. Each computer type had its own terminal technology. Mainframes had terminal technology indicated by a number: the 3270 terminal. These terminals initially worked with green letters on a black background and could hold as many as 32 lines of 80 characters. We still refer to these 3270 terminals as green screens.

Modern mainframe applications no longer use these terminal interfaces. Most often, Applications on the mainframe do not even have a user interface. They only expose services, or APIs, to mid-tier or front-end applications. (See 'Modern mainframe application architectures'.)

Therefore, the need for these green screens is limited today. Only special system administration and application programming tools still have low-level interfaces, and even those are being replaced by tools with more modern interfaces.

Windows system administrators use the "DOS" command prompt, and Unix techies use the Terminal sessions. Similarly, the "green screen" 3270 terminal exists for mainframe techies. (Actually, the Unix Terminal and Windows Command Prompt are rudimentary compared to the 3270 interface to z/OS. The 3270 interface is "full-screen," whereas most Unix and Windows terminals are line-oriented.)

Green Screen Applications: The Technical Debt of Legacy Systems

The days of relying solely on green-screen business applications are long gone. If your organization still depends on them, it's time to consider a change. Modernizing your systems is no longer optional; it's essential for staying competitive and efficient.

The good news is that well-architected green-screen applications can be transformed into modern, service-oriented applications. The old green-screen user interface can be replaced with a contemporary front-end, such as a browser-based solution, making the application more accessible and user-friendly.

However, not all green-screen applications are easy to modernize. Some may be poorly designed or so tightly locked that opening or modifying them is difficult. For these cases, integration with newer systems becomes crucial. I'll discuss how to connect these legacy applications with the rest of the world in a separate section, Integration technologies.

For now, let's focus on the tools and scenarios that still require 3270 screens, and why they continue to depend on this traditional interface.

TSO

What the command prompt is for Windows, and the Shell is for Unix, the TSO tool is for z/OS: a command-line interface that lets you run commands to the operating system to get things done on the computer.

This is a powerful but often cumbersome interface, like the DOS command prompt and the Unix shell. To provide a more user-friendly interface, IBM built the tool ISPF on top of TSO.

ISPF

Another abbreviation I will not expand. You need to know that ISPF is a standard part of z/OS. This tool gives users, nowadays mostly system administrators, a very powerful interface to z/OS.

The editing function and its dataset list utility are the most used functions in ISPF. With the screen-oriented file editor, you can edit the z/OS datasets. The dataset list utility lets you find the datasets on your z/OS system.

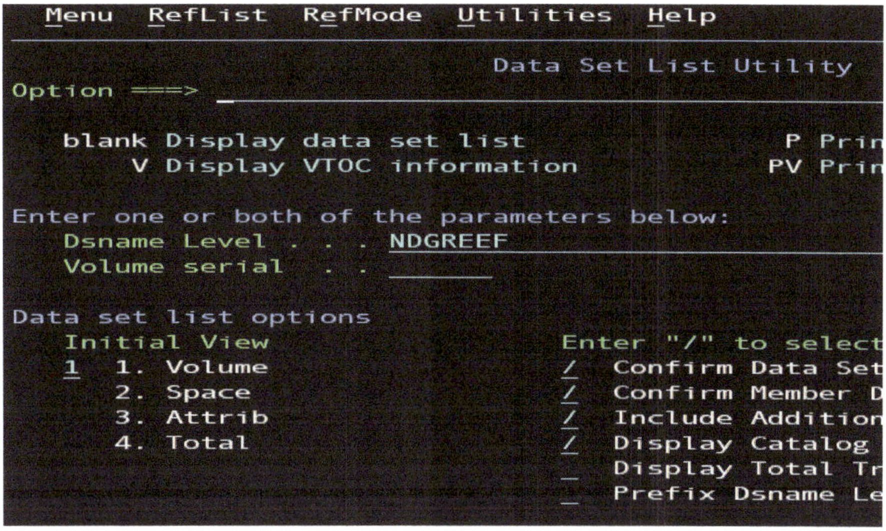

Figure 18 ISPF Data Set list utility

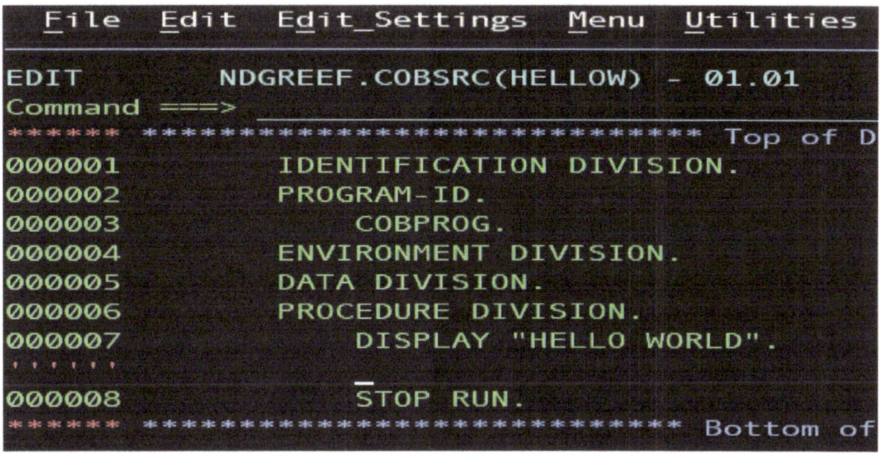

Figure 19 ISPF editor

ISPF also provides facilities to extend its features through a programming interface. Many tool vendors include ISPF tools built on these extensions in their tool installations.

SDSF – or equivalent

SDSF is a separate product from IBM that provides extensions to ISPF. This product, or an equivalent from another vendor, is an essential tool for system and application administrators of z/OS installations. SDSF allows support staff to operate z/OS, manage the processes running on z/OS, examine the output from processes (jobs), and inspect application and system logs. It is like Windows' Task Manager.

SDSF is an IBM tool, but there are tools with equivalent functions from other software vendors, such as IOF, SYSVIEW, or (E)JES.

Modern tools for development and operations

In the previous section, I explained that green screen interfaces still exist for administrative tasks. Yet modern tools with contemporary interfaces also exist for this kind of work. You can manage z/OS and almost all middleware running on z/OS with web-based tools, Eclipse-based tools for z/OS, or, increasingly, Visual Studio Code-based tools for z/OS. Furthermore, you can execute many administrative tasks on z/OS using external tools through REST APIs. More and more development and operations functionality will be available only in this modern tool set.

z/OS Explorer is the standard Eclipse-based tool for z/OS from IBM that you can download for free. It is a desktop client that interacts with z/OS. Many mainframe tools and middleware solutions provide plug-ins for this tool.

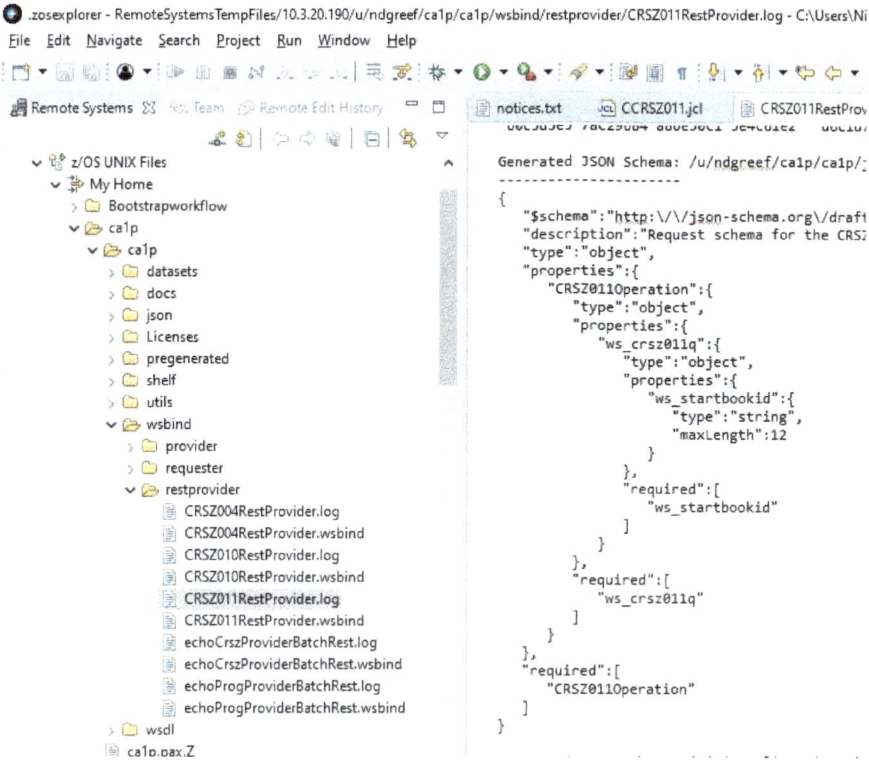

Figure 20 z/OS Explorer

There are several contemporary options for development tools for the mainframe. IBM has developed an Eclipse-based tool called IBM Developer for z/OS (IDz). The software company Compuware (now BMC) has a set of tools for mainframe development called Topaz. There are also open-source tools and plugins, like the IBM Developer for z/OS on VS Code.

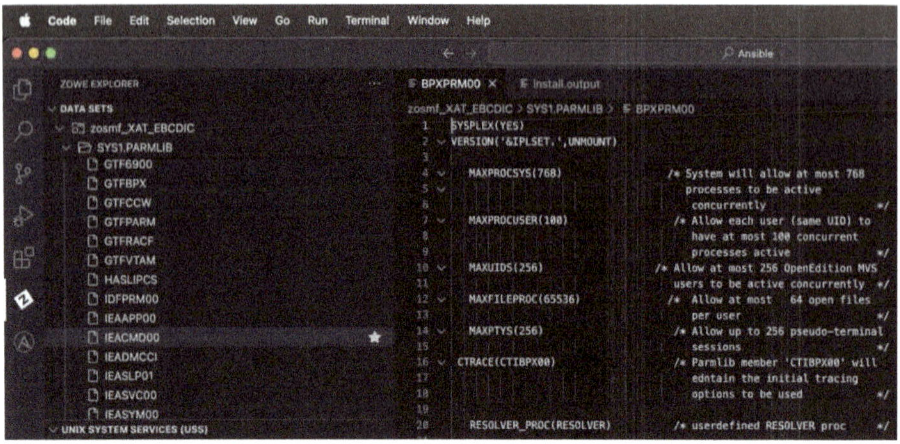

Figure 21 Using Visual Studio Code for z/OS

These modern tools provide a development experience for z/OS applications that is the same as for applications in other languages and on other platforms, such as Java, PHP, or Python. The tools support the development and debugging of mainframe languages such as COBOL and PL/I, as well as Java. Just as important, the tools provide plugins for interacting with middleware such as Db2, MQ, CICS, and IMS.

IBM, Broadcom, BMC, and other vendors also offer many modern tools for administering specific middleware software.

Finally, a recent development is the open-source project Zowe. This project collaborates with several mainframe software vendors. It aims to provide a modern open-source software framework for development and operations teams to securely manage, control, script, and develop for z/OS, similar to other cloud platforms. The Z Open Editor I mentioned earlier is one of the open-source tools developed by the Zowe project.

In separate chapters, I will discuss the modern application development and operations architecture and tools for z/OS, as well as the modern z/OS monitoring architecture and tools.

Chapter 7 Middleware for z/OS

A wide variety of middleware tools are available for the z/OS operating system. Some are similar to software available on other platforms, like WebSphere Application Server, MQ, and Db2. Some are more obscure and only available on the mainframe, like IMS and IDMS. This chapter highlights several key middleware tools for z/OS.

Application Servers

Application Servers are tools that facilitate the creation and operation of interactive applications. Today, we call these tools Application Servers, but on the mainframe, these were traditionally called Transaction Managers. The following is a small intermezzo to explain the similarities and familiarize you with the terminology.

Application Servers and Transaction Managers intermezzo

Despite their different names, Application Servers and Transaction Managers achieve the same goal: making it easy to build and run interactive applications. So, how do they compare?

A platform for deploying and running business applications

Application Servers gather a set of common functions for interactive applications. These functions include network communication, transactional functionality, application scaling, recovery, database connectivity, logging, and much more.

To take Java as a reference again, the Java language has a standard for several functions in the Java Enterprise Edition (JEE), now called Jakarta EE. The z/OS Transaction Managers, such as IDMS, IMS, and CICS, provide similar functions across multiple programming languages, including COBOL, PL/I, C/C++, and Java.

The user invokes a business service through a function identifier

With a modern web application server, the user enters a URL to run application code on that server. For example, a user types the URL in his browser: http://acme.com/fireworks/index.HTML. In this URL, acme.com is the server's name, and fireworks/index.HTML refers to the code to execute on that server – the URI. The application server takes the URI, executes the code, and returns an HTML response page.

Traditional transaction managers work similarly. First, you must connect your terminal to the transaction manager. Then, you type in a transaction code. The transaction code is like the URI in a web application: it identifies which piece of code to run. The transaction manager knows which program to run for this transaction code, executes it, and returns a response screen to the user.

Many organizations no longer use this 'green screen' interface for business applications. Instead, they use a modern web interface for users, and the application functions through the SOAP or REST interfaces that modern transaction managers offer.

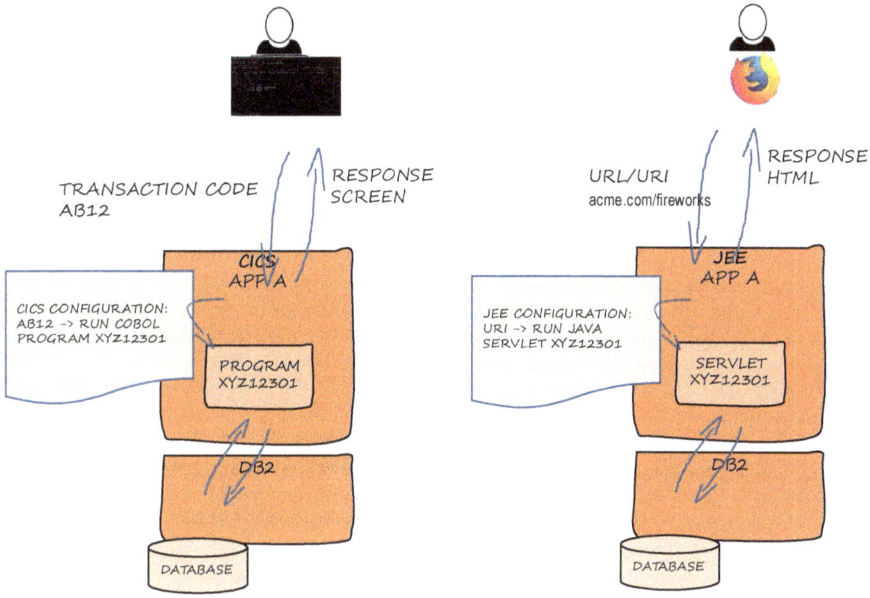

Figure 22 CICS traditional versus a web application server

Now, let's look at what sort of application servers we have on the mainframe.

WebSphere Application Server

IBM's WebSphere Application Server (WAS) is an application server for Java applications that conforms to the JEE Java Platform, Enterprise Edition (JEE) standard. It was one of the first implementations of a Java application server and was also made available on z/OS.

Initial implementations of WebSphere Application Server (WAS) on z/OS were often inefficient and prone to instability. However, with a complete redesign and the introduction of specialty engines dedicated to Java processing (see the section on Specialty Engines), z/OS has evolved into a highly cost-effective platform for running JEE applications and Java workloads (for a deeper discussion on mainframe costs, see Chapter 15).

WebSphere Liberty

IBM WebSphere Liberty is the evolution of IBM's application server technology, offering a lightweight, highly modular alternative to the traditional WebSphere Application Server. Where 'WAS traditional' was always quite heavy, Liberty has much faster startup times, needs less memory, and is more flexible. It maintains full Java EE compliance while allowing developers to include only the features required for specific applications. Liberty is better suited to modern application development practices, with stronger support for technologies such as containers and microservices.

On z/OS, Liberty also runs on the specialty processors for Java, making the platform even more attractive for enterprise Java workloads.

CICS

CICS is IBM's most widely used transaction manager on z/OS. Originally designed for COBOL and PL/I applications, it now also supports Java. CICS remains a cornerstone for high-volume transaction processing in enterprises.

IMS

IMS, another IBM transaction manager, shares many similarities with CICS but also includes a built-in database management component. While less common than CICS, IMS is still critical for core business processing in large organizations. Originally developed for NASA's Apollo moon missions, IMS consists of two main parts:

- IMS/TM (Transaction Manager): Functions as an application server, supporting COBOL, PL/I, and Java—much like CICS.
- IMS/DB: A database management system, covered later in the section on database technologies.

IDMS

IDMS, owned by Broadcom, is a transaction manager and network database system similar to IMS. It consists of two main components:

- IDMS/DC: The transaction manager and application server, functionally comparable to CICS.
- IDMS/DB: A network database management system, which I'll cover in more detail in the Database Management Systems section.

IDMS remains a key solution for organizations relying on network database architectures and robust transaction processing.

ADABAS and NATURAL

Natural is Software AG's fourth-generation programming language, designed for both online and batch applications. Like CICS, it supports interactive transaction processing, but it also enables batch program execution. Natural functions as an application server, typically using Adabas as its backend database management system. It remains a powerful tool for developing and modernizing business applications on mainframe and distributed platforms.

IDEAL and Datacom

Another widely used combination on mainframes is Datacom/DB and IDEAL, both now owned by Broadcom. IDEAL is a fourth-generation programming environment designed specifically for Datacom/DB, a relational database management system. IDEAL generates COBOL code that runs on the CICS application server, using Datacom/DB as its backend database. While initially built for Datacom/DB, IDEAL later expanded to support IBM Db2, offering flexibility for organizations modernizing their mainframe applications.

Database management systems

This section briefly describes the leading database management systems for z/OS. All of these exploit z/OS sysplex capabilities to form a highly available database cluster.

Db2

Db2 for z/OS is IBM's flagship relational database management system (RDBMS) for the mainframe. It organizes data in tables and supports querying through the SQL language. Db2 is widely used for its flexibility, scalability, and robust performance in enterprise environments.

IDMS/DB

IDMS/DB, owned by Broadcom, is a network database management system. Unlike relational databases, it organizes data as a network of relationships, offering modeling advantages and high-speed data access. However, programming for IDMS/DB can be more complex than for relational systems. Data is queried using the CODASYL language.

IMS/DB

IMS/DB is IBM's hierarchical database management system, where data is structured in tree-like hierarchies. While this model provides fast and efficient data access, it can be more complex to program compared to relational databases. IMS/DB uses DL/I (Data Language/I) for data manipulation.

Datacom/DB

Datacom/DB, also from Broadcom, is a relational database management system designed for mainframe environments. It supports SQL and integrates with tools like IDEAL for application development.

ADABAS

Adabas, developed by Software AG, uses an inverted list data model to organize and access data. Data is stored in Adabas files, which consist of data fields and logical records. This model enables efficient data retrieval and is often used in high-performance transactional environments.

Special topic: IBM Db2 Analytics Accelerator (IDAA): Boosting Mainframe Analytics

The IBM Db2 Analytics Accelerator (IDAA) is a specialized appliance designed to enhance the performance of analytical queries on the mainframe. Functioning as an LPAR on the mainframe server, the IDAA offloads complex or resource-intensive analytical queries from Db2 for z/OS, allowing them to run faster and more cost-effectively.

How IDAA Works

As illustrated in Figure 23, the IDAA extends the capabilities of Db2 for z/OS. Data in Db2 is continuously synchronized with the IDAA through a dedicated synchronization process, ensuring that the IDAA always has up-to-date data to process analytical queries efficiently.

Without the IDAA, Db2 for z/OS would handle all queries, both transactional and analytical, using its traditional relational database engine. While relational databases such as Db2, Oracle, and Microsoft SQL Server excel at transactional workloads, they are less optimized for analytical processing. Heavy analytical queries can slow down transactional operations, impacting performance and responsiveness.

The IDAA Advantage

The IDAA provides a unique solution by integrating analytics capabilities directly with Db2 for z/OS. When a query is issued, Db2 automatically determines whether to execute it locally or route it to the IDAA for processing. The IDAA then executes the query and returns the results to Db2, which delivers them to the user or application, transparently and seamlessly.

Key Benefits

The benefit of the IDAA is clear: you can create a single, unified solution for querying your databases. It efficiently handles:

- Transactional queries, which require fast execution and involve small amounts of data.
- Analytical queries, which analyze large volumes of data and demand high-performance processing.

This approach ensures that transactional workloads remain fast and efficient, while analytical queries benefit from accelerated processing, all without requiring changes to existing applications or user workflows. The IDAA effectively bridges the gap between transactional and analytical processing on the mainframe, delivering performance and efficiency where it matters most.

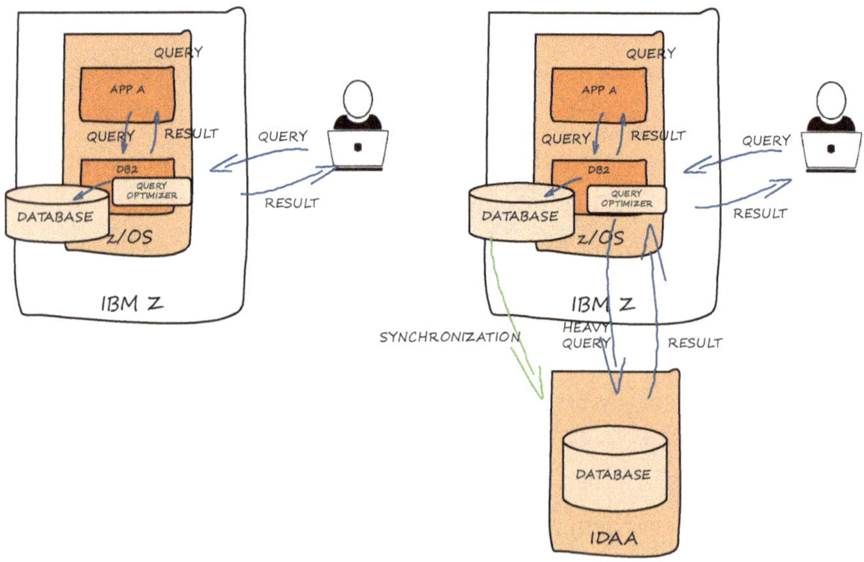

Figure 23 IBM Db2 Analytics Accelerator

Batch processes and the Job Scheduler

Batch processing is an essential application type for many organizations. Batch processes are application processes that process a bundle of input, typically files, in one go and produce a grouped bundle of output, usually files or database tables. This way of processing contrasts with interactive processes, in which a single, user-initiated input is processed, and a result is returned.

Batch processes execute tasks in several steps, and different batch processes depend on one another and must execute in a specific sequence. This kind of processing may become complicated and time-critical in complex organizations. In larger organizations, you can expect a need to run tens of thousands or even hundreds of thousands of batch processes daily.

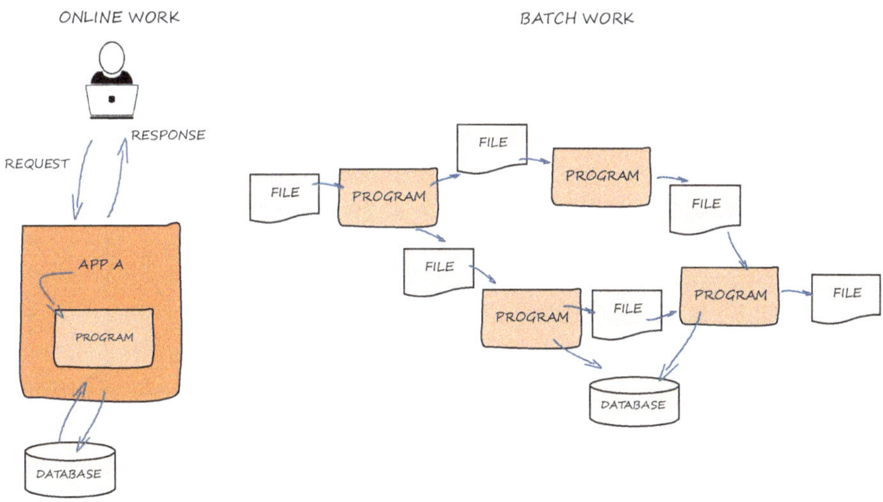

Figure 24 Online and Batch workloads

Since mainframes were initially used mainly for batch processing, you will almost always find a job scheduler on the mainframe. A job scheduler manages, plans, and automates the execution of batch processes.

There are several tools on the market for the mainframe. The most well-known are IBM Z Workload Scheduler (a.k.a. IWS, TWS, OPC/A, and OPC/ESA), CA7, and Beta92.

Integration software

Various tools on the market provide functionality for integrating applications on other platforms with z/OS applications. I will discuss the most generic tools. In Chapter 9, I will discuss more tools, such as middleware-specific adapters.

WebSphere MQ

WebSphere MQ is a well-known messaging solution from IBM. It has the same functionality as MQ on other platforms. With MQ, applications can integrate by exchanging messages, either synchronously or asynchronously.

MQ for z/OS also exploits z/OS sysplex features to create a Queue Sharing Group. In a Queue Sharing Group, multiple queue managers on multiple z/OS systems can share the same message queues. A Queue Sharing Group provides applications using MQ for z/OS with an extremely scalable, highly available messaging solution.

IBM Integration Bus

IBM Integration Bus (formerly known as Message Broker) is a generic application integration tool. Traditionally, these tools were called Enterprise Application Integration tools.

IBM Integration Bus accepts service requests via multiple protocols and formats, transforms input messages into other formats, and orchestrates service processes across multiple service backends with different protocols and formats.

AI and Machine Learning on z/OS

IBM is rapidly advancing the mainframe's AI capabilities, transforming z/OS into a platform for real-time data analysis and intelligent decision-making. AI and Machine Learning on z/OS enable businesses to extract valuable insights from decades of transactional data while maintaining the security, reliability, and governance standards for which z/OS is known. By processing analytics directly where the data resides, organizations eliminate the risks of data transfers, reduce latency, and turn legacy systems into engines for innovation.

In this section, I'll highlight two key AI and ML tools from IBM. (For more on the hardware advancements supporting these capabilities, including the Telum and Spyre processors, see the chapter 'Mainframe hardware.'

Machine Learning for z/OS (MLz)

IBM's Machine Learning for z/OS (MLz) brings machine learning to the mainframe. With MLz, you can develop, deploy, and manage machine learning models entirely within the z/OS environment. It supports all stages, from data preparation to model training, deployment, and monitoring. Data scientists can work with common languages and frameworks like Python, R, and Scala.

AI Toolkit for z/OS

The AI Toolkit for z/OS provides specialized tools for building and deploying AI applications on the mainframe. It includes optimized libraries for deep learning, natural language processing, and predictive analytics, and integrates with popular AI frameworks like TensorFlow and PyTorch. Developers can create neural networks and AI solutions directly on z/OS, while connectors to enterprise data sources provide integration with existing systems.

Together, these tools empower businesses to create and deploy AI and machine learning solutions on the mainframe, leveraging its strengths in security, performance, and data governance.

Chapter 8 Programming languages for z/OS

In the previous chapter, I highlighted the middleware tools on z/OS. In this chapter, I will discuss the programming languages available on z/OS and what to use them for.

COBOL

Sixty years ago, Grace Hopper led the development of the COBOL programming language, intending to make programs portable across different computers.

The principle behind the language was to make computer code much more readable. That is why COBOL has by far the most verbs of all programming languages. The result is that COBOL programs are very legible. Languages like Java and C++ have very technical interfaces and are much less readable. Python is another language that has been successfully designed for readability.

COBOL is a compiled language. That means the code is first translated into low-level machine instructions in so-called load modules before the code can be executed. Other languages, such as Python, Java, or PHP, are interpreted and translated into machine instructions on the fly. The extra step of compilation of COBOL brings a considerable advantage: it is extremely fast compared to interpreted languages.

As per COBOL's readability design point, the language is best usable for business problems (as opposed to scientific or technical problems).

```
IDENTIFICATION DIVISION.
PROGRAM-ID.
    COBPROG.
ENVIRONMENT DIVISION.
DATA DIVISION.
PROCEDURE DIVISION.
    DISPLAY "HELLO WORLD. "
    STOP RUN.
```

PL/I

PL/I was developed in the mid-1960s to create a programming language for business and scientific applications.

The language was developed as a versatile tool with multifaceted purposes, from business applications to operating system development. The language is a bit messy, probably due to the plethora of purposes attempted to be fulfilled.

Like COBOL, the programmer must compile PL/I programs into executable load modules.

```
World: Procedure options(main);
       Put List( 'Hello world' );
       End World;
```

Assembler

Assembler is a programming language that tells the computer which CPU instructions to execute at the lowest level. It is still widely used by organizations running z/OS. In the past, business applications were sometimes developed in Assembler. You should not do that now, but many legacy assembler programs still exist in many mainframe shops.

The advantage of programming in assembler is that it is super fast. The task of programming itself, on the other hand, is very challenging. Assembler programs are notoriously difficult to maintain.

Programmers used Assembler to implement tricks that enabled them to achieve the impossible with the standard operating system or regular programming languages. This practice has created a problematic legacy of technical programs in many mainframe application portfolios.

A typical example is that programmers often used self-modifying code in mainframe Assembler to optimize performance or dynamically adapt program behavior. This technique involves a program altering its own instructions while running. For instance, a typical pattern was to replace a conditional branch instruction with an unconditional branch once a specific condition was met, effectively "short-circuiting" further checks and improving execution speed.

The operational risk of assembler programs

The modern stance is that Assembler programs are a severe legacy. People who can maintain Assembler programs are very scarce, and Assembler programs are also vulnerable to changes in the operating system and middleware software.

On z/OS, we find Assembler programs in modifications to the z/OS operating system and middleware. z/OS offers several ways to customize its behavior. These so-called 'exit points' or 'exits' typically have interfaces only in Assembler. Like application programs in Assembler, z/OS exits in Assembler are a continuity risk. Exits are a risk because nobody knows how to program in Assembler anymore and because these exit points use interfaces that IBM may (and wishes to) change at any time.

Software vendors are removing these Assembler-based exit points and, where needed, replacing them with configuration parameters.

The bottom line is that removing all home-grown Assembler programs from your z/OS installation is highly recommended.

Here's a Hello World program written in IBM mainframe assembler, for all time's sake.

```
TEST0001 CSECT
*******************************************
* This program is Hello Word in assembler *
*******************************************
         STM   14,12,12(13)
         BALR  12,0
         USING *,12
         ST    13,SAVE+4      You can have comments in the
code
         LA    13,SAVE        Like this
         WTO   'HELLO WORLD!' Write text to log
         L     13,SAVE+4
         LM    14,12,12(13)
         BR    14
SAVE     DS    18F
         END
```

Fortran

FORTRAN is a programming language designed for scientific and engineering purposes. It is still a pretty popular programming language for these purposes.

```
program hello
  ! This is a comment line; it is ignored by the compiler
  print *, 'Hello, World!'
end program hello
```

Java

In the 1990s, a team at Sun Microsystems created the Java programming language, designed to run on any device. By the early 2000s, Java support was extended to mainframe systems.

Java programs are not compiled in the traditional sense; instead, they are interpreted by the Java Virtual Machine (JVM) at runtime. However, Java's execution on mainframes remains less efficient than that of languages like COBOL and PL/I. Under traditional licensing models, this inefficiency can make running Java costly.

To address this, IBM introduced zIIP specialty engines, which offload eligible Java workloads from general-purpose CPUs. Since Java processing on zIIPs does not contribute to software license charges, this approach significantly reduces the cost of running Java on mainframes—despite its lower execution efficiency. See more on mainframe costs in Chapter 15.

```
void main() {
    println("Hello World");
}
```

C/C++

In the 1990s, C/C++ was introduced to z/OS, becoming a mainstream choice for developing mainframe applications and tools. The process of compiling a C source program into a load module closely resembles that of COBOL and PL/I.

```
#include <iostream>
using namespace std;

int main()
{
    cout << "Hello, World!";
    return 0;
}
```

JCL

JCL (Job Control Language) is the original "scripting" tool for the mainframe. While IBM has added some programming-like features over the years, JCL remains far from a full-fledged programming language.

Its quirky syntax reflects its origins: JCL was designed for punch card readers, a legacy still visible today. Its core purpose is simple—to launch programs or sequences of programs.

Many of JCL's idiosyncrasies have outlived their practical use in modern z/OS environments but persist for backward compatibility. Given that tens of thousands of batch jobs can run on a mainframe, managing thousands of JCL "programs" becomes inevitable.

Yet, there's a clear need for a more accessible, readable, and modern alternative. Perhaps something akin to Python?

```
//JOBNME5  JOB AB123,PRGRMR,NOTIFY=MYUSER1,MSGLEVEL=(1,1),
//         CLASS=1
//RUN          EXEC PGM=COBPROG <- PROGRAM TO RUN
//* PROGRAM WAS PUT IN HERE --v
//STEPLIB  DD DISP=SHR,DSN=MYUSER1.LOADLIB
//SYSPRINT DD SYSOUT=*
```

Rexx

The story goes that an IBM developer, Mike Cowlishaw, created the Rexx programming language, fed up with the only available scripting language, CLIST. In one night, he is said to have developed Rexx. His colleagues were enthusiastic when he showed it to them the next day.

On z/OS, Rexx fulfills the same role as Unix scripts in Unix environments. System administrators mostly use it to automate all administration tasks, as many operating system functions are accessible from Rexx.

You can run Rexx interactively under TSO/ISPF and use it in batch jobs.

I find that Rexx is somewhat similar to PHP in terms of flexibility. Both languages support dynamic typing and do not require explicit variable declarations, making them well-suited for quick, flexible coding—though this also comes with similar drawbacks.

```
/* Main program */
say "Hello World"
```

Unix shell script

z/OS includes a Unix subsystem that complies with POSIX standards and supports a command shell, as in any Unix flavor. With the shell scripting language, you can automate all Unix processes. The most commonly used *bash* shell flavor is ported to z/OS.

You can also run Shell scripts in batch jobs.

```
#
echo "Hello World"
```

SAS

Many z/OS users use the SAS language from SAS Institute. Besides its analytical capabilities, SAS is used for ad hoc programs and reporting.

SAS is often used on the mainframe to process measurement data generated by z/OS and to create various usage and performance reports.

```
proc ds2 libs=work;
data _null_;

  /* init() - system method */
  method init();
    declare varchar(16) message; /* method (local) scope
*/
    message = 'Hello World!';
    put message;
  end;
enddata;
run;
quit;
```

Easytrieve

You can also regularly find the programming language Easytrieve from Broadcom in z/OS environments. Application support staff use Easytrieve to create ad hoc programs, and advanced end users use it to generate business reports from application data.

Python

Python is an emerging programming language for z/OS. IBM and Rocket Software have created a z/OS-compatible version of Python. For z/OS-specific functions, IBM has created Python utilities that simplify their execution on the z/OS platform. This product is IBM Z Open Automation Utilities (ZOAU). Pronounce that abbreviation.

Other languages

There are many other languages available on z/OS. However, the ones discussed here are the mainstream languages. Languages like Python and R are emerging for analytical applications; the programming language Go from Google, JavaScript for Node.js, PHP for web applications, and Perl for scripting.

Augmenting traditional COBOL and PL/I code with Java

Not all these languages for z/OS operate on language islands. IBM has developed language interoperability, especially for the traditional languages COBOL and PL/I and the traditional application servers IMS and CICS, primarily with Java. This interoperability means you can combine COBOL and PL/I code with Java.

Now, you can modernize your applications in Java while keeping the functionality you have developed over the past decades in COBOL or PL/I. You can navigate towards more Java-based developments while keeping your investment in COBOL or PL/I functionality.

In the following section, I will highlight the options offered by the languages COBOL and PL/I, as well as those provided by the IMS and CICS application servers.

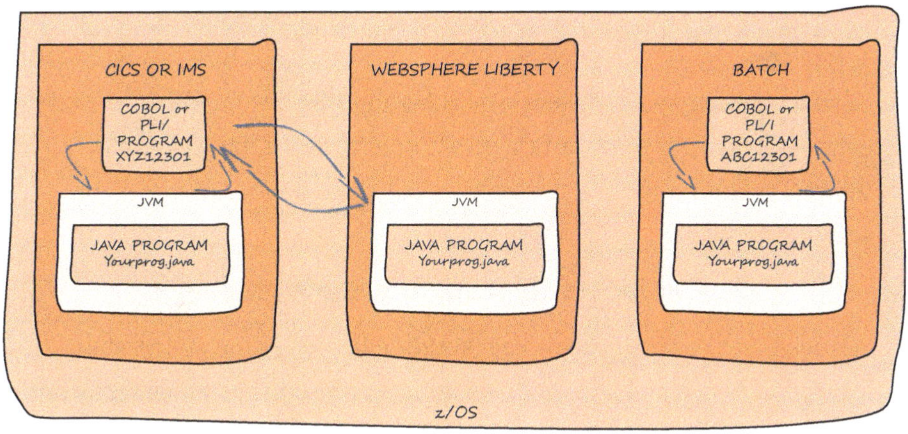

Figure 25 COBOL and PL/I interoperability with Java

Batch COBOL and PL/I to Java

COBOL and PL/I for z/OS have built-in features to call Java from COBOL and vice versa. These features have become significantly more manageable over the last few years. Before, some glue code was needed, but nowadays you can do without it and minimize the code that bridges the COBOL or PL/I peculiarities with Java's peculiarities.

Interoperability of COBOL and PL/I with Java under CICS and IMS

In the CICS and IMS application servers on z/OS, you can mix COBOL and PL/I code. You do not normally use the native COBOL or PL/I facilities for these. Instead, you use the CICS and IMS facilities to call Java from COBOL and PL/I programs and vice versa.

The first option for both CICS and IMS is to run "Java Standard Edition" (Java SE) programs inside the CICS and IMS servers in combination with COBOL or PL/I. This option provides basic Java facilities in combination with COBOL or PL/I.

The second option, also applicable to both IMS and CICS, is to use a WebSphere Liberty JVM server for Java. The Liberty JVM offers significantly more functionality than Java SE and is more focused on web technology.

The technology used differs for CICS and IMS because the CICS and IMS technologies differ a lot, but the functionality is similar. Using the Liberty JVM, the second option is generally considered a more modern and strategic approach.

Guidance: Selecting the Right Language

Choosing the appropriate programming language for mainframe development depends on the use case, performance requirements, and long-term maintainability. Below is a breakdown of when to use each language:

COBOL and PL/I

Use for:

- Stable, high-performance transaction processing (e.g., core banking, insurance, or financial systems).
- Extending or maintaining existing functionality in legacy applications.
- Scenarios where predictability, reliability, and low-latency processing are critical.

Java

Use for:

- Developing new application functionality, especially when integrating with modern technologies (e.g., microservices, Kafka).
- Projects requiring scalability and cross-platform compatibility.
- High-volume transactional applications (similar to CICS/COBOL/Db2 environments).

Note: Ensure your team has experienced Java developers familiar with performance tuning and resource optimization. Building high-performance Java applications, in general, demands deep expertise, much like traditional COBOL/CICS environments.

Python

Use for:

- Ecosystem and utility functions that are non-business-critical but require rapid development or frequent updates.
- Operational management tasks, such as automation, monitoring, and IT workflow orchestration.
- Scenarios where high lifecycle frequency (e.g., frequent script updates) is expected. Avoid for core transactional systems where performance and stability are paramount.

Rexx and Shell Scripts

Use for:

- Low-level, system-specific functions that are not feasible in Python or lack support in Ansible collections for IBM Z.
- Quick automation tasks or ad-hoc system administration where lightweight scripting is sufficient.

C/C++, SAS, Easytrieve

Use for:

- Highly specialized use cases, such as legacy reporting, data extraction, or analytics, where no viable alternative exists in the languages above.
- Scenarios where existing SAS/Easytrieve scripts are deeply embedded in workflows and rewriting them would be cost-prohibitive or risky.

This structured approach ensures that each language is used where it excels, balancing performance, maintainability, and modernization goals.

Chapter 9 Integration technologies for z/OS

Many mainframe applications began as monolithic systems, with minimal need for external integration. When cross-organizational data exchange was necessary, it was typically handled through file transfers.

The 1990s marked a shift as client-server applications emerged, demanding real-time integration with legacy mainframe systems. This era saw the development of specialized tools and facilities to bridge z/OS applications with new client-server environments. By the 2000s, the rise of loosely coupled architectures further expanded the possibilities for integration.

This chapter explores the spectrum of integration tools available on z/OS, from traditional screen-scraping solutions to modern approaches supporting REST APIs and Kafka.

File interfaces

The mainframe was designed for batch processing. Therefore, integration via files is traditionally straightforward and well-catered.

You can use multiple options to exchange files between applications on z/OS and other platforms.

Network File System

Network File System (NFS) is a standard protocol that you can use to create a space for sharing files between applications on different platforms. Although NFS was initially used mainly with Unix, it is now a part of most other operating systems, including z/OS. Nowadays, NFS solutions are often not preferred in larger organizations due to security and availability challenges.

FTP

The File Transfer Protocol (FTP) is a standard protocol to send files over a TCP/IP network to a receiving party, and it is also supported on z/OS. With FTP, you can use a script or program to transfer a file as part of an automated process. FTP can be made very secure with cryptographic facilities. FTP comes in a few flavors, of which SFTP is the most used flavor.

FTP is part of most operating systems, including z/OS.

Managed File Transfer

Managed File Transfer (MFT) is a specialized facility for sending files over a network, offering advanced capabilities that go beyond basic file transfer. The term "Managed" reflects its enhanced features, which significantly improve reliability, security, and operational efficiency.

MFT solutions automate and streamline file exchange processes by providing strong encryption and robust authentication, integrating with security repositories, offering automated retry mechanisms for failed transfers, and delivering detailed reporting and comprehensive APIs.

On z/OS, several MFT solutions are available as standalone products. IBM offers Connect:Direct and MQ-FTE, Broadcom provides NetMaster File Transfer and XCOM, and BMC delivers Control-M. Additionally, z/OS supports integration with open, distributed MFT frameworks such as Apache Camel.

Message queueing

Message queuing is a general method for applications to communicate point-to-point. With message queuing, applications stay decoupled, reducing their dependence on each other's availability and response times. Applications can operate at different times and communicate over networks and systems that may temporarily be down. As we will explore in the next section, applications and intermediate infrastructure must be available to enable effective application communication when using alternative point-to-point protocols such as web services.

The basic notion of message queueing is that an application sends a message to a queue, and another application asynchronously reads messages from that queue and (optionally) responds with another message. Beyond the specific asynchronous nature of message queueing, a significant advantage is that it can ensure message delivery: messages will not be lost, and when the infrastructure is unavailable, they remain stored until they can be delivered.

IBM MQ is one of the best-known and most robust message queueing solutions available on z/OS. IBM MQ also supports Java Message Service (JMS), an open messaging specification for Java applications.

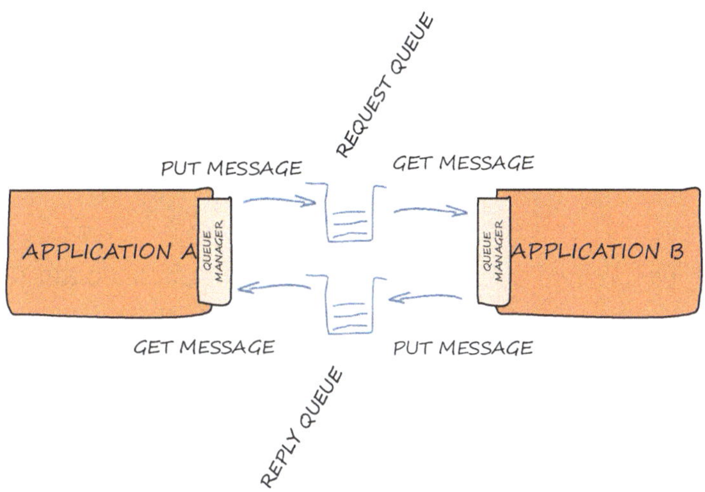

Figure 26 Applications using Message Queueing

Web services (SOAP, REST)

Web services technology represents the modern approach to enabling application communication over the HTTP protocol, the same protocol used for web browsing. There are two primary types of web services: SOAP and REST.

SOAP, the older of the two, relies on XML, a resource-intensive format due to its complexity. In contrast, REST is more modern, lightweight, and typically uses JSON, making it the foundation of today's API-driven economy.

The key advantage of web services integration is its simplicity: no additional infrastructure is required beyond a capable web application server. Integrations are lightweight and can be loosely coupled, offering flexibility and scalability.

However, web services have a notable limitation: the HTTP protocol does not guarantee message delivery, unlike message queueing systems. Applications that use web services must implement their own recovery and retry mechanisms to handle connection loss.

Most modern z/OS application middleware, such as CICS, IMS, WebSphere Application Server, and IDMS, now supports both REST and SOAP interfaces. Yet native full-functional REST API capabilities are often limited on platforms such as CICS, IMS, and IDMS, largely for commercial reasons. To bridge this gap, additional tools are required to build REST APIs for COBOL applications. IBM's z/OS Connect serves this purpose, enabling seamless integration. For more details, see the section on Adapters.

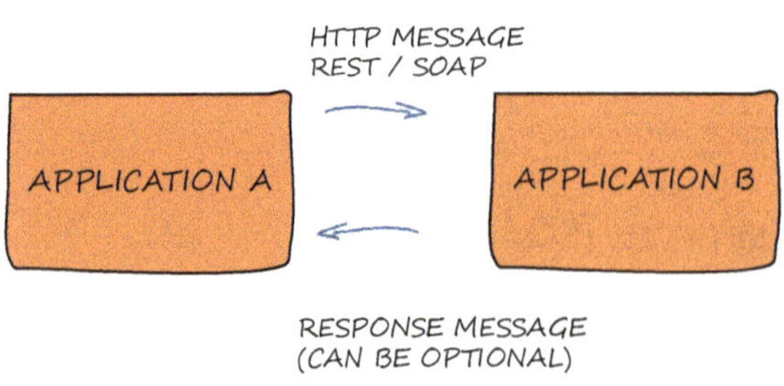

Figure 27 Applications using Web Services

Event streaming

Event streaming is another approach to integrating applications. Through event streaming, an application can publish events that other applications may be interested in, and can subscribe to events from other applications.

Apache Kafka

Apache Kafka, usually referred to as Kafka, is the de facto standard, open-source event streaming platform. An example of the use of Kafka is when a CRM application serves as the system of record for customer data. Other applications may be interested when, for example, the address of a customer changes. Instead of asking the CRM application for valid customer address data every time it is required, other applications can subscribe to an 'address-update' event and record or cache the latest customer address.

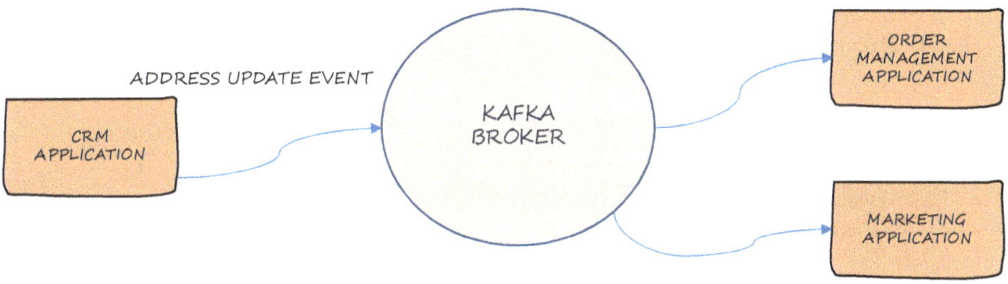

Figure 28 Example of application integration with Kafka

Native Kafka programming interfaces and Kafka Connect

Applications can interact directly with Kafka to publish or subscribe to event updates. As a Java-based solution, Kafka naturally provides a Java programming interface. However, it also supports other languages natively, including Python and Scala.

To extend Kafka's reach to z/OS, IBM introduced a Kafka SDK for COBOL, enabling COBOL applications to integrate with Kafka. Additionally, software company RVS-Systems developed a tool called zKafka Connector, a native z/OS solution built on the z/OS Language Environment. This approach further simplifies Kafka integration for z/OS applications.

The open-source Kafka project provides functionality for programming languages and applications that lack native Kafka support. The Kafka Connect component is created to sit between Kafka and other middleware technologies, such as databases and messaging middleware.

Figure 29 illustrates the use of Kafka Connect on z/OS. In the Kafka Connect solution, z/OS applications can produce events to Kafka by sending messages to MQ. The Kafka Connect component reads these MQ messages and creates events for Kafka topics in the Kafka broker. Similarly, z/OS applications can consume events through MQ. Kafka Connect is configured to subscribe to Kafka events. The received events are turned into messages on MQ queues. Z/OS applications can listen to these queues and process the events.

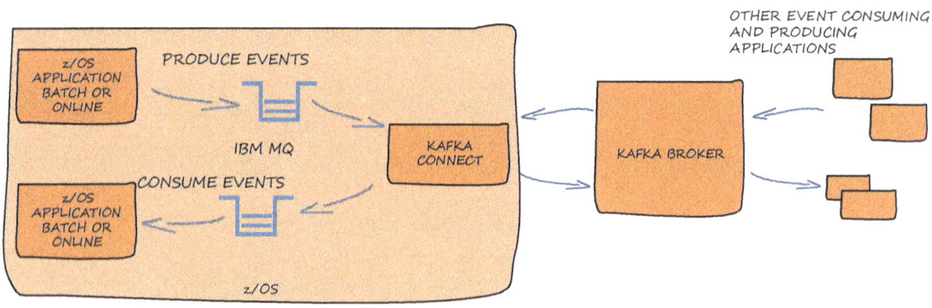

Figure 29 z/OS applications with Kafka Connect and MQ

Enterprise Service Bus

Another form of integration can be achieved through Enterprise Service Bus tools. These tools probably give the widest variety of integration options. An ESB can receive and send service requests using various protocols. The ESB can convert messages between many formats. An ESB can orchestrate complex message interactions between multiple applications. Enterprise Service Bus products are Tibco Substation ES and IBM Integration Bus.

ESB solutions can run on z/OS, which often offers easier integration with the z/OS application side, and they can also be implemented on a non-z/OS platform and integrated with z/OS agent software.

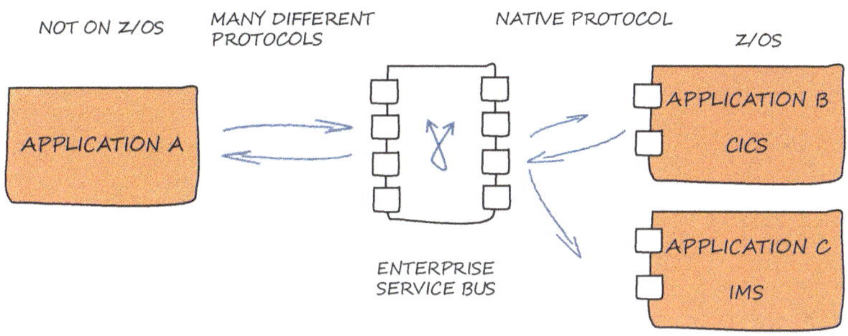

Figure 30 Enterprise Service Bus

Adapters

In many cases, it may be impossible to refactor your old mainframe applications. The applications may have a bad, unstructured design, middleware technology may have limited options, skills may not be available, or the risk of changing existing applications is too high. There may also be other reasons you do not want to touch the application code.

Application adapters can help open applications in these situations. Generally, an adapter converts a proprietary middleware protocol, such as a CICS, IDMS, or IMS interface, into a more common API or generic protocol, such as a Java program, a web service, or a message queueing interface. Some adapters also provide the option of converting a proprietary 3270 screen interface into a neat API through screen scraping.

I will highlight a few of the types of tools here.

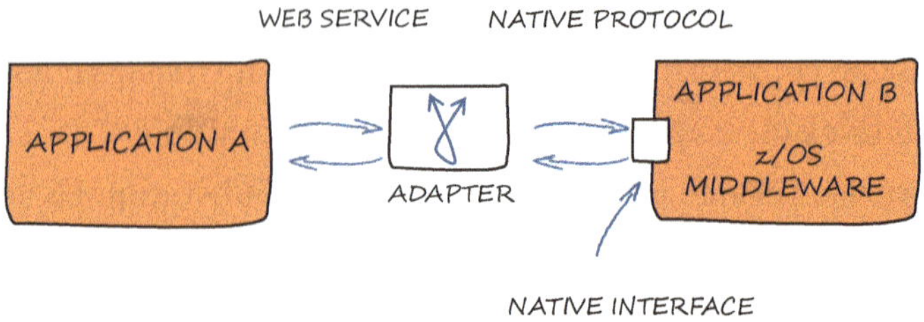

Figure 31 Generic functioning of an adapter

CICS Transaction Gateway

CICS Transaction Gateway provides an API for Java and C programs to call a CICS transaction on z/OS.

With CICS Transaction Gateway, it is not possible to do the reverse: invoke an external program from CICS. CTG Only enables external programs to call CICS.

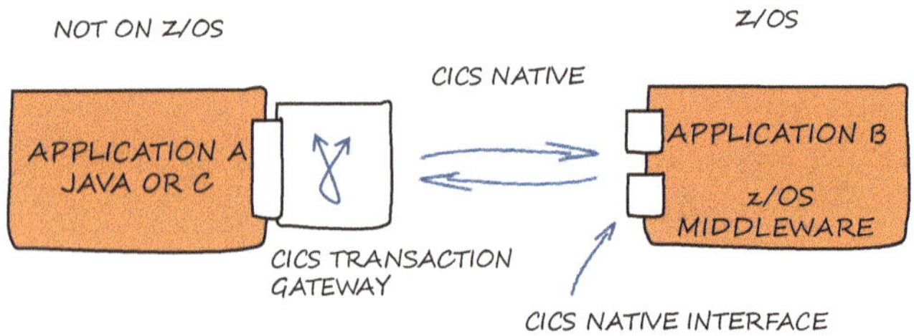

Figure 32 CICS Transaction Gateway adapter

IMS Connect

IMS Connect provides a Java API for invoking IMS functions from Java programs. Through it, you can access IMS transactions and data in IMS DB (see the section Middleware for z/OS). As such, IMS Connect functions similarly to CTG, though the native interfaces differ.

REST API enablement tools

IBM's z/OS Connect is a well-known tool for enabling REST API integration on z/OS. It acts as a bidirectional adapter, allowing you to expose existing z/OS assets such as CICS transactions, IMS calls, Db2 operations, and MQ interactions as RESTful APIs. Conversely, it also enables z/OS applications to call external REST APIs, bridging modern and legacy systems.

Beyond z/OS Connect, other tools and approaches for REST API enablement on z/OS include Broadcom's API Gateway, Software AG's Adabas & Natural REST Adapter, and Rocket API.

Open-Source Frameworks: Tools such as Apache Camel and Spring Boot can be used with z/OS to build custom REST APIs, though they may require additional middleware or integration layers.

These tools collectively provide flexible options for modernizing z/OS applications and enabling seamless integration with cloud, mobile, and web-based systems.

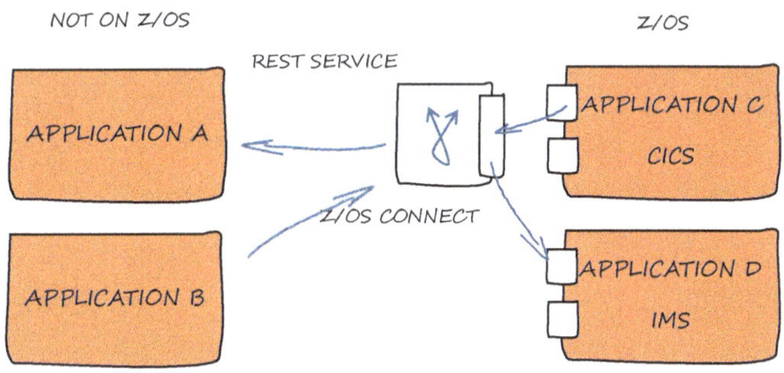

Figure 33 The z/OS Connect adapter

Screen scraping tools

You may have old legacy applications built as a silo, with only 3270 user interfaces and no decent program interfaces. If you need to reuse the functionality in these legacy applications in new applications, you face a significant challenge. For this problem, screen-scraping tools can be a last resort.

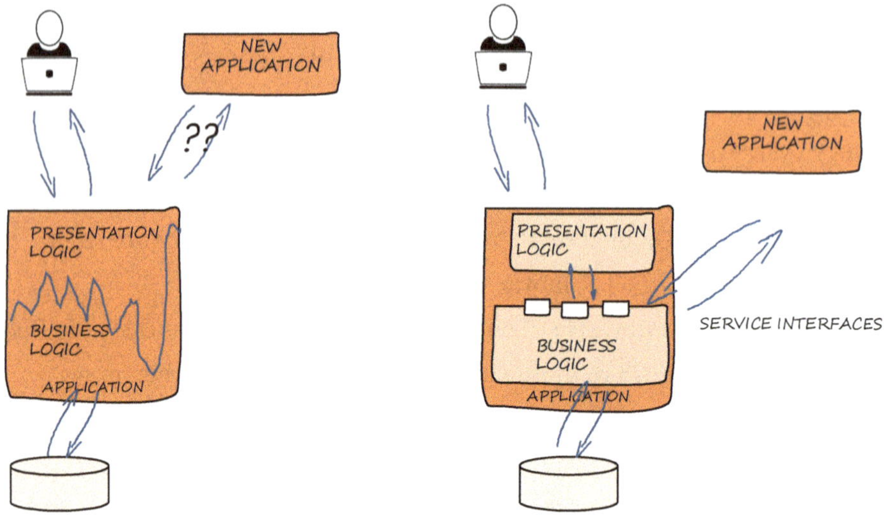

Figure 34 An application silo – refactoring is the ideal solution

A screen-scraping tool can simulate the interaction of a business user with the old application's user interface. The tool automates the end-user's workflow by programmatically filling in the old application screen. This automation allows the tool to aggregate and expose these interactions to higher-level services. Other applications in your organization can invoke these higher-level services through a modern API, such as a web service.

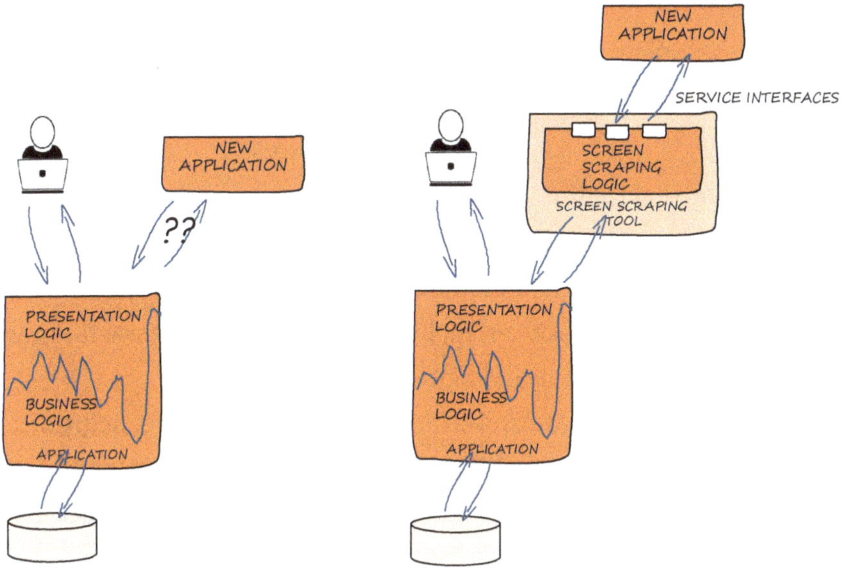

Figure 35 Integration with a screen-scraping solution

Products like HostBridge, Rocket LegaSuite, and IBM Host on Demand provide screen-scraping facilities.

Screen scraping does not make the problem go away

The big problem with screen-scraping integrations is that you have a more complex application landscape and even more development artifacts you need to maintain. Not only do you have the old application to support, but you also need to manage the screen-scraping middleware and logic.

Screen-scraping should temporarily solve a severe issue in your application landscape. Even today, solutions are built on top of modern web applications using screen scraping. Today, people call these “robots” to make them seem modern, but such robots have the same problems as screen scraping from 3270 terminal screens.

The bottom line is that screen-scraping solutions are only a temporary solution at best. You should replace them with modern integration technology and modernize the application as soon as possible.

Legacy integration suites

Many integration tools on the market provide one or more of the adapter types discussed earlier, enabling seamless connectivity between legacy z/OS applications and modern systems. These tools specialize in bridging native z/OS interfaces, including screen-based interactions, with contemporary applications and platforms.

For instance, GT Software and Oracle Legacy Adapter offer solutions that allow businesses to integrate CICS, IMS, Db2, and other mainframe assets with modern applications. Their adapters support a range of protocols, such as REST and SOAP, and help organizations modernize their infrastructure without replacing core mainframe logic. By facilitating communication between z/OS and cloud, web, or mobile environments, these tools extend the value and usability of existing mainframe investments.

Database access via JDBC, ODBC

So far, we have discussed application integration through application interactions – applications calling one another.

Direct database access

Applications on non-z/OS platforms can alternatively directly access data in databases on z/OS through the standard data access protocols ODBC and JDBC. All suppliers of database software for z/OS provide ODBC or JDBC drivers.

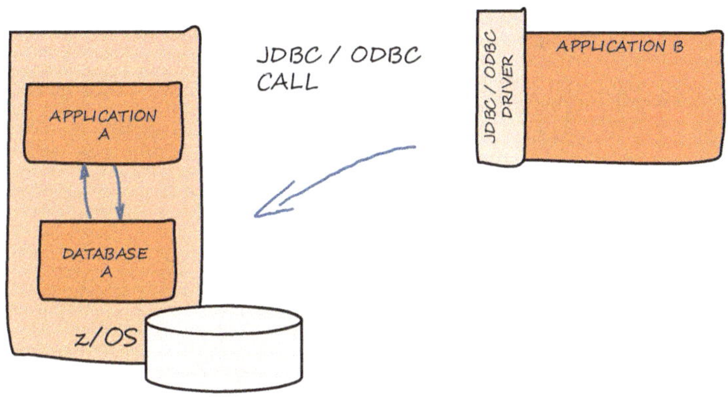

Figure 36 Integrating with JDBC and ODBC

Access via a data virtualization layer

Data virtualization layers provide an abstraction over diverse data sources.

Applications on distributed platforms can alternatively access z/OS data, whether in Db2 for z/OS, IMS, or other non-relational sources, through a virtualization layer. Through a virtualization layer, a virtual view is established using standard protocols such as JDBC/ODBC, REST/JSON, and others, without moving, replicating, or transforming the source data.

Tools that provide these services include Tibco Data Virtualization and IBM Data Virtualization Manager.

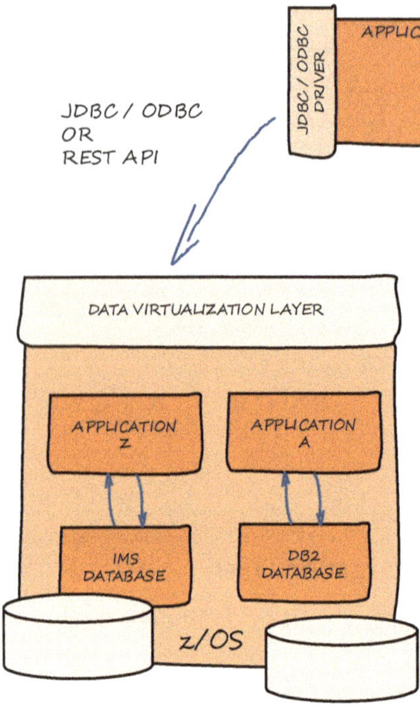

Figure 37 Integration through a data Virtualization Layer

Architectural alternatives to direct database integration

From an architectural perspective, directly accessing another application's data is not an ideal approach to integration. This practice leads to tightly coupled, siloed applications, which are notoriously difficult to maintain and scale. As applications become increasingly dependent on shared data models, even minor changes can create cascading complications.

Beyond maintenance challenges, direct data access introduces concurrency risks, where conflicting application requests at the database level can lead to inconsistencies or severe performance bottlenecks.

A more sustainable approach is to encapsulate data access behind service interfaces, ensuring that applications manage their own data while interacting with others through well-defined APIs. This aligns with the principle of loose coupling, fostering flexibility, scalability, and easier long-term maintenance.

What's Next

So far, we've explored z/OS: its middleware, languages, and integration capabilities. But the mainframe isn't just z/OS. In the next chapter, I'll step outside the z/OS world to explore Linux on IBM Z, which will wrap up our discussion of the underlying technology. After that, I'll return to discuss modern capabilities and strategic decisions. But first, let's see what happens when you run Linux and all its containerized, cloud-native possibilities on mainframe hardware.

Chapter 10 Linux for the mainframe

In the early 2000s, IBM ported the Linux operating system to the mainframe server hardware. This critical development opened the mainframe for various applications and tools. In this chapter, I will discuss how to run Linux on the mainframe. You will see that this is mostly very similar to Linux on other platforms.

In the "Mainframe operating systems" section, I mentioned two ways to run Linux on the mainframe: as a separate operating system in an LPAR or virtual machine or as a Linux container inside z/OS.

The first section of this chapter will highlight the option of running Linux 'natively' as a separate operating system on mainframe hardware. The second section will describe the option to run Linux in containers natively under Linux, and under z/OS. Next, I will talk about OpenShift, the management tool for Linux containers. Finally, I will discuss the benefits of Linux on IBM Z and what it can bring to your organization.

Linux on IBM Z

Linux for the mainframe is officially called Linux on IBM Z. Many users refer to it as zLinux. Linux on IBM Z is no more or less than a regular Linux distribution for any other server hardware.

Several supported Linux distributions for the mainframe are available: Red Hat, SUSE, Ubuntu, Debian, AlmaLinux, and Rocky Linux.

What does a Linux mainframe configuration look like

A typical Linux on IBM Z setup uses the z/VM hypervisor (see the section "z/VM, the mother of all hypervisors") or the open-source KVM hypervisor to manage the usually larger number of Linux instances needed. The hypervisors are functionally similar to VMware or KVM for x86 servers: They provide logical hardware environments where operating systems and applications can run in virtual machines.

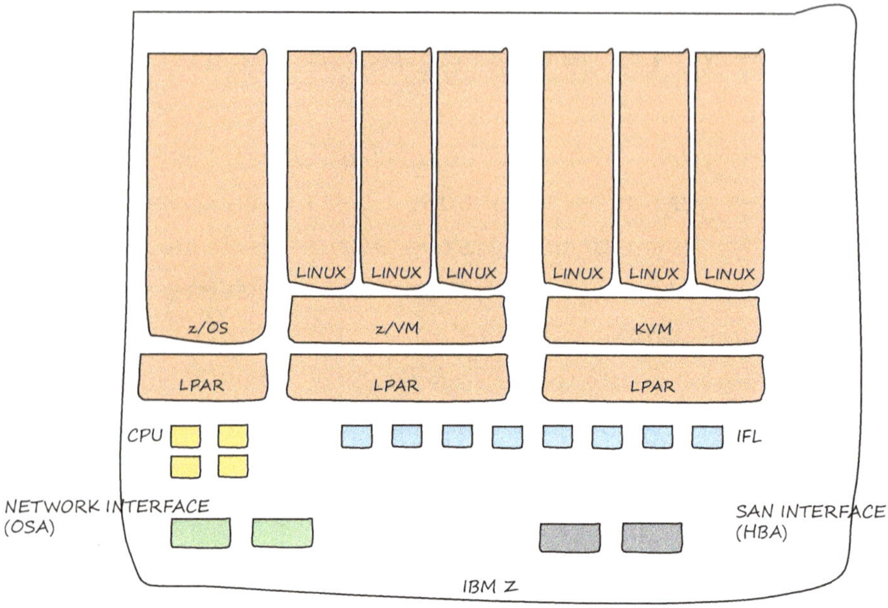

Figure 38 An overview of virtualization with Linux on Z

Typically, for Linux servers on IBM Z, one or more LPARs are configured to run z/VM or KVM. These LPARs use the IFL specialty engines, CPUs specifically configured for Linux, in the mainframe hardware. The z/VM or KVM hypervisor virtualizes the CPU and memory resources, allocating them to the Linux instances. Additional hardware resources, such as memory, network, and storage interfaces, are also virtualized and configured for the Linux instances.

Linux containers on IBM Z

With the popularity of the Linux platform, the number of Linux servers in an organization has quickly grown. This growth came with a manageability issue. Installing and servicing such a Linux server farm became an increasing hassle. Linux containers are a revolution for the

Linux platform that makes running and servicing Linux applications much easier.

Linux containers are lightweight packages that combine an application and its technical Linux dependencies—an entire runtime environment—in one. Because they are lightweight and portable, containers allow faster development and flexibility for changing requirements and needs.

On IBM Z, you can run Linux containers in two ways:

1. A pure Linux environment with Linux containers in their virtual machine(s).
2. Linux containers within the z/OS operating system using the z/OS Container Extensions.

In this section, I will describe both options on a high level.

Linux containers with Linux on z

The first way to run Linux containers on IBM Z is by using a native Linux solution. In this configuration, the KVM hypervisor runs in a logical partition (LPAR) on the IBM Z server, where it serves as the container engine for Linux containers that run applications.

This setup is similar to container solutions on other platforms, with the only difference being the underlying hardware, the IBM Z architecture itself.

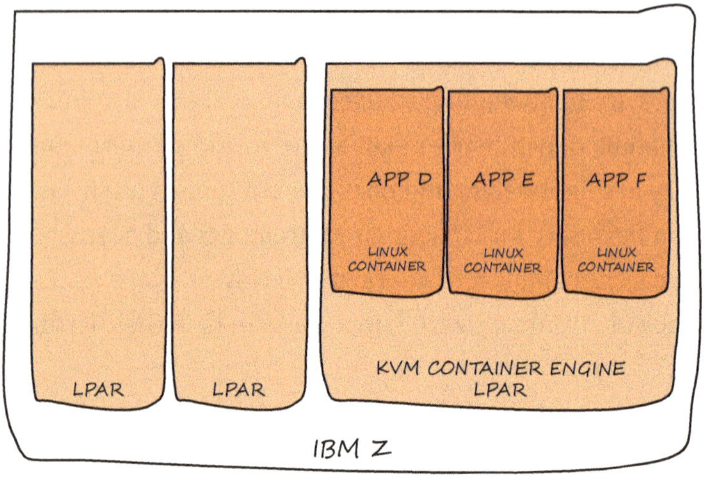

Figure 39 Linux containers in a native Linux configuration on IBM Z

Linux hosted on z/OS with z/OS Container Extensions

We'll switch to an alternative method for running Linux applications on the mainframe: z/OS Container Extensions.

What is z/OS Container Extensions

z/OS Container Extensions (zCX) allow z/OS users to run Linux containers as part of the z/OS operating system. With this infrastructure, you can run containerized Linux applications in the same environment as traditional z/OS COBOL or PL/I applications. How zCX runs Linux containers in a z/OS address space is illustrated in Figure 40. In a zCX address space, you can run multiple Linux containers.

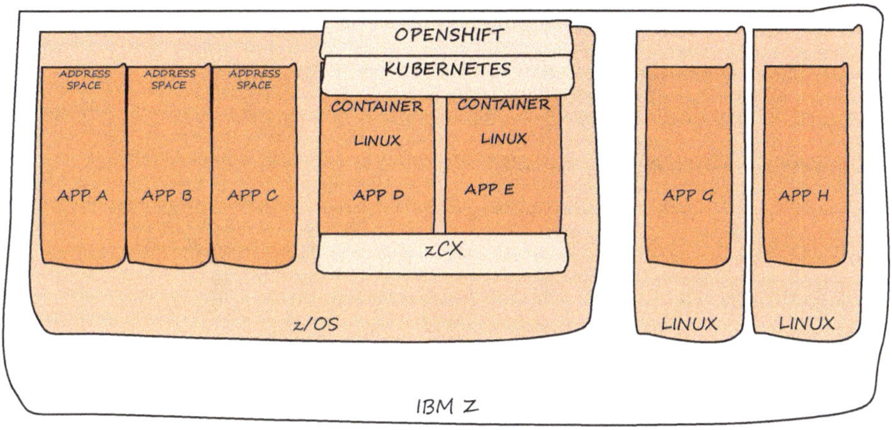

Figure 40 Containerized applications on z/OS with zCX

Why run Linux inside z/OS?

The zCX's container runtime facilities allow the mainframe to use Linux containers while exploiting the z/OS platform's extreme availability and scalability.

The value of running Linux containers on z/OS lies in the possibility of reusing the system management, security, and high-availability facilities of z/OS. These values are best expressed for applications and tools that can only run on Linux but have a strong relationship with applications and infrastructure running on z/OS. Instead of running tools on distributed Linux machines or on separate Linux on Z LPARs, you can now run these applications as part of the z/OS installation.

The benefit of using this facility is that processes and tools for system management, automation, monitoring, and disaster recovery can be reused directly from existing z/OS facilities. This significantly reduces management effort for Linux applications.

OpenShift

The Linux container concept was developed to address the manageability challenges associated with large numbers of Linux servers. However, as the use of Linux containers has grown, a new level of manageability concerns has emerged: overseeing even larger numbers of containers. It is now common to encounter hundreds or thousands of Linux containers within an IT landscape.

In recent years, several tools have been created to address this challenge, with Kubernetes and OpenShift emerging as the most prominent technologies in this field.

Kubernetes is an open-source platform designed to automate the operations of Linux containers. It simplifies many of the manual processes involved in deploying, managing, and scaling containerized applications. Kubernetes enables you to schedule and run containers across clusters of physical or virtual machines. Its architecture divides a cluster into components that work together to maintain the cluster's defined state.

OpenShift, built on top of Kubernetes, extends its capabilities by providing a comprehensive platform for managing large-scale Linux container environments.

What is Linux on Z good for?

Mainframe hardware is expensive, so why consider running a commodity operating system like Linux on a non-commodity mainframe server?

I am aware that platform discussions can quickly become contentious, and I want to avoid turning this into a debate. Instead, I will explain as objectively as possible why running Linux on the mainframe might make sense for your organization. Not every argument will apply equally to every organization, but I will focus on two key considerations: cost and operational efficiency.

Reduce cost through consolidation

In the chapter "Mainframe hardware," I mentioned that IBM Z hardware is highly scalable and designed to support numerous operating system instances. A Linux configuration on IBM Z can exploit this scalability, enabling you to run many Linux instances on a single IBM Z server. This configuration makes Linux an excellent platform for consolidating Linux applications.

Running many Linux instances on a large mainframe server makes it cheaper to run and maintain that Linux configuration. Why?

- You need fewer servers and, therefore, fewer connectivity devices for networks and storage. This ends up in a more straightforward configuration that is easier to maintain.
- Linux on IBM Z is a green solution. A single IBM Z box's power consumption is lower than that of equivalent x86 servers, and an IBM Z server can handle much higher utilization levels.
- Data center floor space can be reduced when consolidating on IBM Z, reducing facility costs.
- Consolidating more Linux servers on an IBM Z server can reduce software costs. The number of CPUs in a server often determines the cost of software licenses. Reducing the number of CPUs can reduce software costs. Some organizations have migrated solely to Linux on IBM Z to reduce their software bills.

Run Linux apps with z/OS within the appropriate management organization

One less obvious benefit of running specific applications or tools on Linux within the mainframe is the organizational perspective. If you have Linux applications that closely relate to some of your z/OS applications, it may be advantageous to host these Linux applications on the mainframe.

Often, for these applications, software lifecycle management must occur in sync with z/OS applications and middleware, and it is most efficiently operated within the context of z/OS application and infrastructure management. Many larger organizations face technical coordination and planning challenges when running these applications on the standard Linux platform. The Linux for x86 department frequently has tools that differ from those needed in a mainframe environment. Finally, the culture is typically different. Enterprise Linux teams often manage significantly more Linux servers with less specific requirements, faced with a much more diverse set of users and needs. The mainframe-related applications on Linux on IBM Z often present a considerable burden.

The dynamics and approach are different; hence, it is often better for both parties to have a looser relationship. Linux for x86 and Linux for Z management can still share best practices and tools, but the Linux platforms are often best managed within the dynamics of their ecosystems.

Running these z/OS-related applications or tools on Linux for Z may benefit your organization. Managing these applications in the mainframe ecosystem is more efficient.

In summary: Linux on Z

This chapter has explored two distinct ways to leverage the open-source Linux ecosystem on mainframe hardware.

The first approach is to run Linux natively on IBM Z, which closely resembles running Linux on x86 hardware. This configuration combines the flexibility and agility of Linux with the reliability, security, and scalability of IBM Z hardware, making it an attractive option for organizations seeking to modernize their infrastructure while retaining the strengths of the mainframe.

The second approach is to run Linux containers on z/OS, integrating Linux workloads directly into the z/OS environment. This method not only preserves the functional benefits of Linux but also adds the non-functional advantages of z/OS, such as its robust security, high availability, and resilience.

The introduction of Linux containers on z/OS is likely to drive a shift in how organizations deploy Linux on IBM Z, particularly in environments where Linux is used as part of z/OS-related components. For these workloads, running Linux containers directly on z/OS may prove more efficient than deploying them on a separate Linux on Z instance, which requires a dedicated hypervisor and additional hardware resources within the mainframe configuration.

Additionally, platforms like Red Hat OpenShift can further enhance the deployment of Linux containers on IBM Z. OpenShift provides a Kubernetes-based container orchestration platform that simplifies the management of containerized applications at scale. When deployed on IBM Z, OpenShift enables organizations to seamlessly integrate Linux workloads with their existing z/OS environment, leveraging the mainframe's strengths while adopting modern DevOps practices and cloud-native architectures.

By combining Linux on Z, Linux containers on z/OS, and OpenShift, organizations can create a flexible, scalable, and future-proof infrastructure that bridges the gap between traditional mainframe strengths and modern cloud-native innovation.

Back to z/OS

Now that we've explored what Linux brings to the mainframe platform, I will step back into z/OS territory. Whether you're running Linux containers or traditional z/OS applications, development practices matter. In this chapter, we'll examine how modern development methodologies, such as DevOps, agile practices, and automated testing, are transforming how teams build and maintain z/OS applications.

Chapter 11 Application development for z/OS

This chapter will present both traditional and modern views of the software development and operations (DevOps) processes for z/OS. The ideal situation is not there yet, but significant progress has been made over the past few years to transform the traditional waterfall-oriented processes and tools for developing applications on z/OS into a modern-day agile way of working. I will examine the development processes and discuss some supporting tools available on z/OS.

Traditional DevOps process for development

Traditional software development followed a waterfall process. Nowadays, we develop software using agile methods in smaller, more iterative steps.

The traditional waterfall is a staged process

Applications developed on z/OS typically follow a structured lifecycle consisting of four stages: Development, Testing, Acceptance, and Production.

In the Development stage, the application is created and undergoes unit testing within the Development environment. Once unit testing is complete, the application advances to the Testing stage for integration testing. If successful, it proceeds to the Acceptance stage, where it undergoes acceptance testing. Finally, upon approval, the application is deployed to the Production stage, marking its go-live in the Production environment.

Each stage is tied to a dedicated environment, reflecting a waterfall-oriented development approach. For example, an application in the Testing stage uses the Test environment to validate its functionality. However, this process introduces challenges, particularly in source code management, as parallel development efforts can create conflicts.

Additionally, the rigid alignment between the development process and physical infrastructure can limit flexibility and agility.

Deployments are incremental - the concept of a build does not exist

What is also different in the traditional development process compared to modern ideas is that the concept of an application build did not exist. A build today is a collection of all the application artifacts needed to run an application in a runtime environment. You need an executable and, typically, configuration files, scripts, and definitions to run an application.

On the mainframe, we get an executable program through a compilation process. An application also requires some runtime definitions and scripts to function. For z/OS, these are artifacts such as JCL scripts, property files, database definitions, interface definitions, etc. In short, we call all these artifacts a build package or a build.

Most of the processes to create the different z/OS application artifacts comprising an application were disparate and unique in the traditional waterfall process. Some technologies allowed standardizing build processes for specific components, mainly for code compilation. However, most processes were either manual or automated, using in-house tools and whatever technology the organization considered best at the time.

Limitations of the Waterfall Model in Mainframe Development

The waterfall model, with its lengthy development cycles, was once the standard for application development, and the DTAP (Development, Testing, Acceptance, Production) setup effectively supported traditional workflows (see Figure 41). However, this approach has become increasingly problematic due to its inherent limitations:

The model's rigid, sequential structure makes it difficult to adapt to changing requirements once a phase is complete. This inflexibility results in prolonged project timelines, complicating responses to scope changes or evolving business needs. The heavy reliance on manual processes not only slows development but also increases the risk of errors. Additionally, the infrequency and scale of changes—often large and monolithic—introduce significant risk and operational disruption.

Supporting tools for mainframe development were traditionally limited, focusing primarily on source code management (SCM) for staged environments. Widely adopted tools included Broadcom's Endevor, Compuware's ISPW, and Micro Focus's ChangeMan, while IBM's SCLM—once a free alternative—was discontinued years ago. Although these tools excelled in SCM, they offered little support for build automation or deployment, creating obstacles for teams seeking to modernize their development practices.

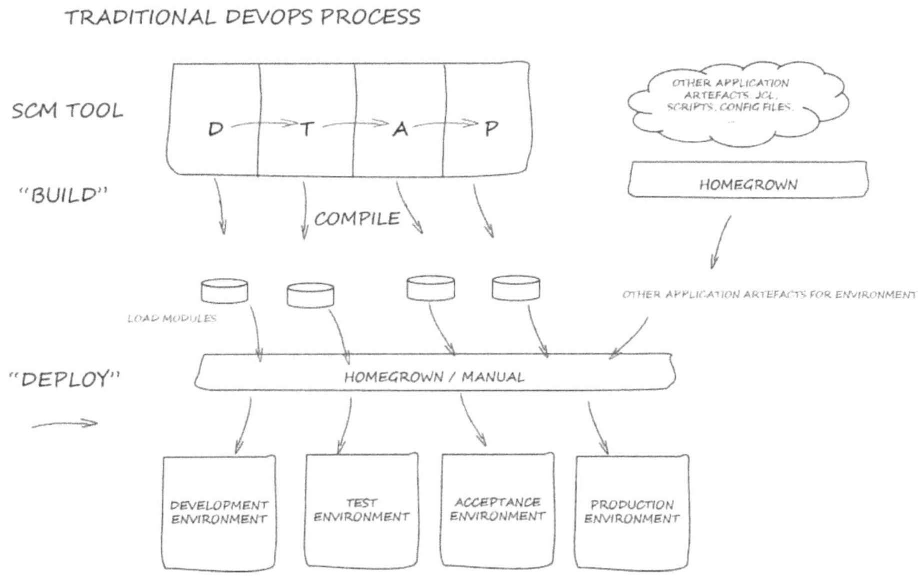

Figure 41 Overview of the traditional development process

Modern development processes for the mainframe

The demands of the development process have evolved significantly. Today, application development and modification must accelerate, with faster change cycles and higher quality standards. This shift led to the rise of Agile development, which emphasizes flexibility, collaboration, and rapid iteration. To meet these modern requirements, automation of build and deployment processes is no longer optional—it is essential.

Principles for mainframe development today

To align mainframe development with Agile practices and the speed required by today's business environment, a set of core principles must be adopted:

- All application artifacts are managed in a Source Code Management (SCM) tool, ensuring version control and traceability.
- Build processes for all artifacts that are fully automated and executed consistently, eliminating manual errors and ensuring reproducibility.
- Deployments are environment-agnostic: A build should contain no dependencies tied to a specific environment or organization, allowing seamless deployment to any target environment.
- Deployment processes are fully automated, including rollback capabilities to revert to previous configurations if needed. These processes are cohesive and apply uniformly across all application artifacts.
- Deployments are repeatable and predictable, ensuring consistency and reliability every time.

These principles are not unique to z/OS; they apply to any modern IT solution. However, given the legacy development processes and tools on z/OS, adopting these principles requires significant technical and organizational changes. Organizations must modernize their workflows, tools, and mindsets to fully embrace Agile mainframe development.

The modern Source Code Management tools for z/OS

The modern SCM tool for z/OS must support all application artifacts. For the mainframe, this means that not only must traditional MVS-type artifacts be supported, such as COBOL programs, COPYBOOKS, and JCL, but also Unix-type artifacts, such as Unix scripts and configuration files in z/OS Unix directories. The tools and processes should allow for EBCDIC-type artifacts to be created for the z/OS runtime environment, as well as ASCII, Unicode, and binary artifacts.

Modern SCM tools that can manage z/OS artifacts include ISPW from Compuware, RTC from IBM, and, of course, Git, whether self-hosted or integrated with GitHub, Azure DevOps, or GitLab.

Automating application builds

The modern DevOps process automates the build process. The build process takes the required versions of the application artifacts from the source code management repository and creates a coherent package of these artifacts. The build package is deployed to a (test) environment.

The build can be deployed in any runtime environment outside your organization. This principle not only enforces the standardization of processes and infrastructure in your IT organization but also enables future deployments in yet-unknown environments.

The automated build process should be callable via a generic API or CLI to be integrated into other automated processes as needed.

Building automation on z/OS can be accomplished with several tools. Some of these tools can handle the z/OS-specific needs. IBM has a few solutions: Rational Build Engine, Jazz Build Engine, and Dependency-Based Build. Other software vendors have similar tools. Compuware has capabilities in ISPW. Broadcom has created tools based on Zowe. All these tools still have some gaps in the coverage of the different artifacts that can make up a z/OS application.

These tools are primarily augmented with open-source tools like Gradle, Maven, Ant, and others.

Automating application deployment

The modern DevOps process for z/OS also automates the deployment of the built application version. The deployment process takes all the artifacts in the build package, customizes them for the specific runtime environment by applying naming conventions and runtime-specific aspects, and deploys them across the different runtime components in the environment. The deployment tools use a flexible model to represent the target environment for deploying an application.

The automated deployment process is callable via a generic API or CLI, which can be integrated into other automated processes as needed.

The most prominent deployment tools available for z/OS include IBM's Wazi Deploy, UrbanCode Deploy, XebiaLabs' XLDeploy, and homegrown solutions using tools such as Jenkins or Ansible. And cloud-based solutions like GitLab and Azure DevOps.

Integration with other processes in the DevOps processes

I have indicated above that the DevOps processes described there must be callable. This requirement is essential since we do not want to automate just the individual pieces of a development process, but the entire chain, the whole lifecycle process.

Only a fully automated Development process can provide optimal development speed. Integrating build and deployment with other methods, such as infrastructure provisioning, test data provisioning, and testing, is critical.

Most of the tools mentioned above have APIs or command-line interfaces that enable integration with CI/CD orchestration tools such as Jenkins and Ansible, as well as cloud platforms such as Azure DevOps and GitLab.

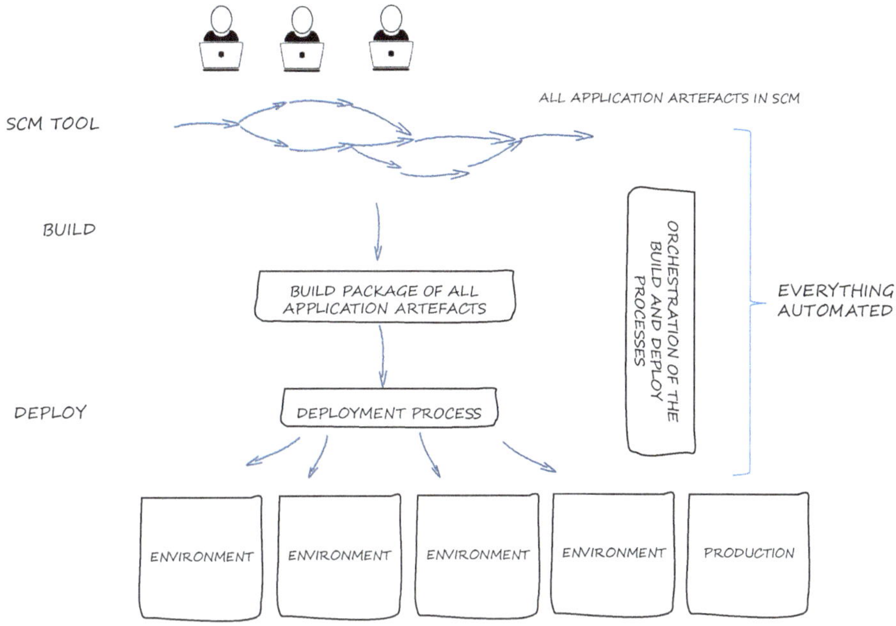

Figure 42 Automated DevOps processes

Some thoughts on full deployments versus delta deployments

The traditional staged development process for the mainframe is based on developing deltas: you only (re)deploy the changed artifacts. In modern application development, it is common practice to deploy complete applications. Deploying full applications generally makes the deployment process easier to manage and better aligns with an application architecture that favors small, loosely coupled applications.

To facilitate agile development in z/OS environments, we should consider moving to a process that supports full application deployments. The old way of working with deltas may not give us the speed and flexibility we need today. Such an approach has consequences in multiple areas:

- Applications should be defined in smaller, independent parts. We might need to reuse some of the best practices from microservices architecture. No technological aspect of z/OS would inhibit such an approach.

- It should be possible to activate (phase in) an application with many more load modules than we are used to today while ensuring that the application continues to run. To facilitate this, mechanisms in the application middleware tools, such as CICS and IMS, will need to be developed.

Enabling such capabilities requires fundamental changes in how we develop and manage traditional mainframe applications. No legacy practice or tool should escape rigorous reevaluation, though.

Case study: A CI/CD pipeline for COBOL applications on z/OS

An organization faced a significant challenge. z/OS was chosen as the platform for a large strategic initiative to run a high-volume, low-latency application. A substantial amount of development work over a few years was required to create a long-term strategic core application for the organization.

The existing development model was largely a waterfall model. It was supported by a toolset designed for the waterfall model, with its drawbacks, such as few and long development cycles, problems with iterative and parallel development, and a lack of agility. The toolset also included several homegrown tools.

As part of preparing to design the new core application in COBOL, the organization redesigned its CI/CD pipeline for COBOL applications. They implemented a contemporary, largely off-the-shelf toolset to realize the pipeline depicted in Figure 43.

The result of this transformation was a CI/CD infrastructure that supported iterative development of COBOL applications and middleware. The organization enabled application teams to shift from 5 to 10 large application deployments per year to 5 to 10 small application deployments per week. By integrating automated testing and code quality analysis into the pipeline, the organization further improved application deployment.

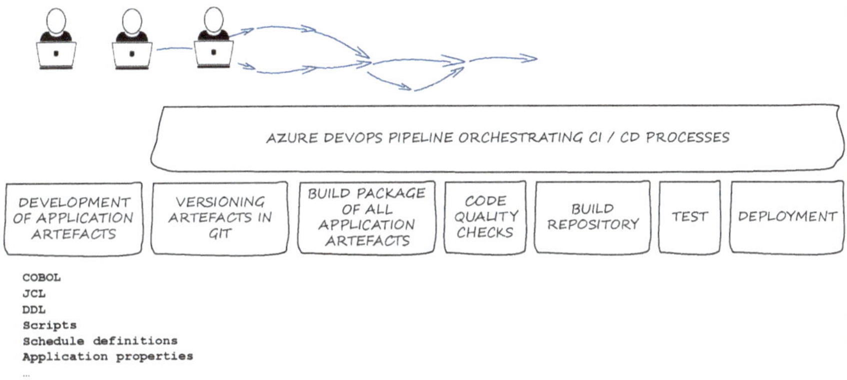

Figure 43 A modern CI/CD pipeline for COBOL applications

In summary: work to do

In many organizations, state-of-the-art DevOps practices for z/OS lag behind other development practices and, in some areas, also technologies. Mainframe users and software suppliers are doing significant work in this space, and both communities should prioritize it to ensure mainframe development keeps pace with the rest of the industry.

Chapter 12 Security on z/OS

Security is an undisputed strength and a distinguishing feature of the mainframe and the z/OS operating system. This section will highlight key security features of the mainframe hardware and the z/OS operating system.

The mainframe's hardware provides several distinguishing security features. In z/OS, a centralized security facility providing authentication and extensive authorization functions is a built-in part of the operating system. Also, z/OS exploits the security features that the mainframe hardware offers. This chapter will highlight the central security facility in z/OS and how z/OS uses unique hardware features of the mainframes.

Centralized security management

The central security management built into z/OS provides a standardized interface for security operations. As we will discuss later, IBM and Broadcom have competing products implementing this interface. Any z/OS platform will need one of these security management solutions.

The SAF interface

z/OS's main security component is the centralized security function called the System Authorization Facility or SAF. This component provides authentication and authorization functions.

The z/OS operating system and the middleware installed on z/OS rely on this central facility. z/OS and middleware software can call SAF functions to validate access to the protected resources.

A protected resource can be a dataset, a message queue, or a database table. It can also be a critical function or command of the middleware software product. By making calls to the SAF interface, the middleware product can validate access to all functions and resources for the many tasks and users on z/OS.

Security products

The z/OS operating system's SAF interface is just a standardized interface specification. Software vendors can implement it for their security management products. The SAF interface does not prescribe how security definitions should be stored or administered.

Three commercial solutions have implemented the SAF interface: IBM offers its security product RACF, and Broadcom offers two tools: ACF2 and Top Secret. All three software products provide additional services for security management, such as administration, auditing, and reporting.

The products all define a unique role in the organization, with the restricted ability to define and change the security rules. The security administrator has these special authorizations. The security administrator determines which users and groups can access specific resources after the resource's System or Business owner approves.

Similarly, a few special tasks require special attributes assigned to users. For example, there is an auditor responsible for monitoring the security guidelines.

Figure 44 The SAF interface and security products

Zero Trust architecture on z/OS

In a z/OS cluster, many applications run concurrently in the z/OS instances in a sysplex. Applications on z/OS share the same compute resources and middleware instances. A significant risk on such a shared platform is that one application can access resources, files, databases, queues, etc., belonging to another application. Moreover, lateral movement in the event of a potential credential breach on a shared platform requires even more attention.

These risks need to be mitigated through measures that ensure the separation of applications on the platform and prevent access to each other's data. In what follows, I will explain how zero trust can be implemented on this shared computing platform of the mainframe. These measures are often referred to as segmentation.

Data in memory protection

Before going into application segmentation, one internal z/OS concept to be aware of in this context is the z/OS Address Space. All infrastructure, middleware, and Application tasks run in their own address space. Address spaces provide the processes with their own protected virtual memory space. The z/OS operating system exploits special hardware features in the IBM Z server, such as storage protection keys, to ensure that processes in one address space cannot access data in another.

Segmentation mechanisms to realize zero trust

Application segmentation is realized on z/OS through the strong security mechanisms provided by the central SAF security facilities. This security feature is unique to z/OS and is designed to implement stringent access control on a shared application platform to ensure accurate isolation of application resources.

Applications running on the same z/OS sysplex should be logically separated through stringent security definitions in SAF, following these principles:

- All application-specific resources (database tables, queues, transactions, files, etc.) are protected with application-specific resource protection profiles.
- Access to application resources is grouped into application-specific functional groups.
- Applications are assigned their application-specific functional accounts.
- Functional users are granted (only – zero trust!) the minimum authorizations needed to perform the business operation required.

Thus, when access is granted to (functional) accounts to use certain application functions through a group, access is granted through application-specific profiles to application-specific resources. Through this mechanism, a logical "application container" is constructed, and a user of the function can access the application's resources. Still, this container cannot provide access to resources in another "application container" by any means, as RACF similarly protects that container.

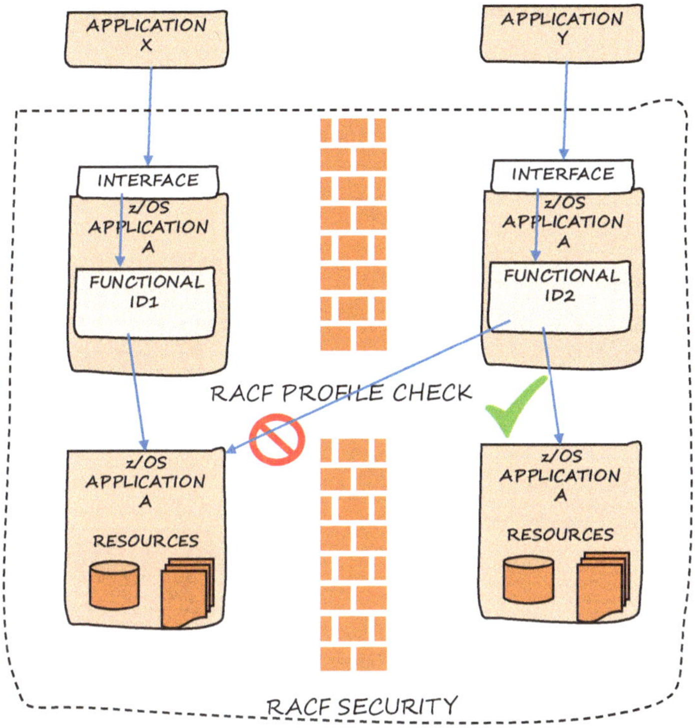

Figure 45 Application segmentation on z/OS with RACF

Multifactor Authentication

Traditional authentication on z/OS relies on a userID/password combination validated against the central security registry, as we have seen with RACF, ACF2, or Top-Secret.

However, a user ID and password authentication is no longer considered sufficiently safe. Multifactor authentication is broadly adopted to address this security issue. On the z/OS platform, multiple software vendors offer multifactor authentication extension products. BMC, IBM, and Broadcom have MFA products in their portfolios. With these products, instead of using the regular password to log on to z/OS, a user must supply a token generated by a special authorized device. This special device can be a SecurID token, a smartphone with a special app, or another mechanism. The critical thing is that next to a user ID and password, PIN code, or fingerprint, there is a second thing – the second factor - needed for the user to prove their identity: the special device or authorized app on your phone.

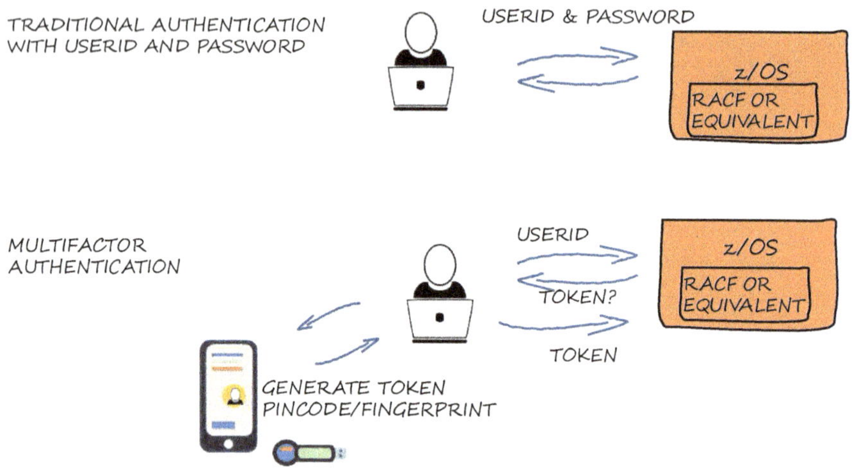

Figure 46 Multifactor authentication on z/OS

Data protection

Access to data on z/OS is protected through the general security facility in SAF. As we saw in the previous section, all application resources are protected through application-specific resource profiles. Access to these resources is prohibited by default. The IBM Z platform provides additional security measures to protect data.

Stored data protection

Physical data in the storage servers can be encrypted, protecting it against physical intruders.

Finally, applications can also implement encryption for individual resources (files, databases, queues, etc.) using cryptographic facilities on z/OS.

Immutable backup facilities

Cyber threats

Everybody is aware that a new challenge has grown in our IT context nowadays: threats from malicious attackers. We have connected our IT systems to the Internet to allow our software systems to interact with our customers and partners. Unfortunately, this has also created an attack surface for malicious actors. Several types of cyber attacks have become a reality today, and cyber threats have infiltrated the realms of politics and war. Any organization today must analyse its cyber threat posture and defend against threats.

One of the worst nightmares is a ransomware attack, in which a hostile party has stolen or encrypted your organization's data and will only restore control after you pay a ransom or meet their other demands.

The last-resort protection against ransomware attacks is to store your data in a secure location that attackers cannot access or manipulate.

Enter Cybervault

A Cybervault is a solution that sits on top of your existing data storage infrastructure and backups. In a Cybervault, you store your data in a way that prevents physical manipulation: you create an immutable backup of your data.

For your mainframe setup, IBM has created a solution for this: IBM Z Cyber Vault. With IBM Z Cybervault, you can add a third leg to the data-mirroring setup of our GDPS configuration, as I described in Chapter Parallel Sysplex. This is an asynchronous copy of the data. From this third copy of our data, the Cybervault software creates immutable copies. In

Figure 47, you can see how the Cybervault solution can extend your GDPS configuration from Figure 17.

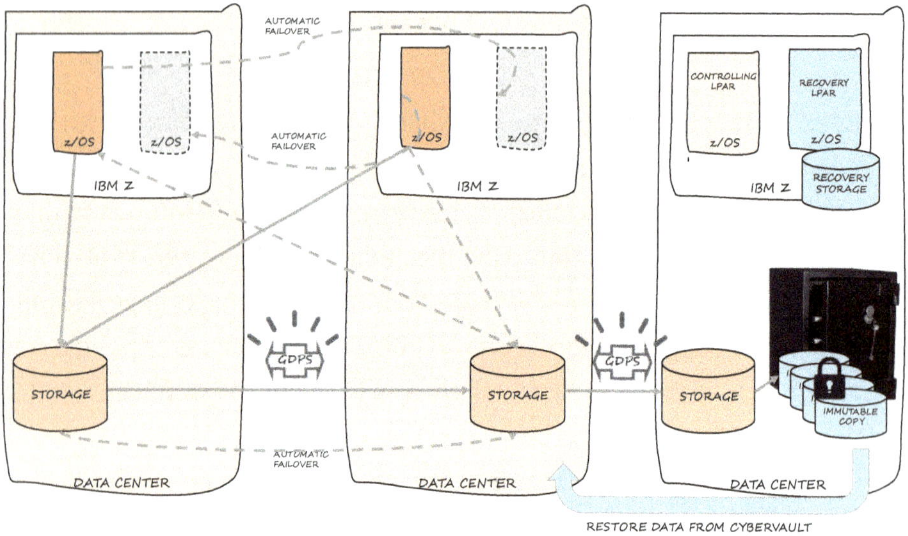

Figure 47 IBM Cybervault extends the GDPS configuration

This solution combines IBM software and storage hardware. With IBM Z Cyber Vault, we can make a copy of all our data at regular intervals as needed. Typically, you make an immutable copy every hour or so. Some IBM Z users make a copy only once a day. This frequency can be configured. From every immutable copy, you can recover your entire system.

In a cleanroom, a completely separated compute environment, the recovered system can be analysed for data corruptions. Ideally, this is fully automated, and when corruptions are detected, the system alerts management and takes action. Ultimately, data can be restored to the production system. This can be a full restore of all data of an entire parallel sysplex, or a specific selection of data, a surgical restore.

In addition, software vendors have developed solutions that provide specific facilities for surgically recovering certain types of data from the Cybervault. Suppliers like BMC and IBM, for example, provide advanced tools to roll forward data in Db2 or IMS databases in case of a ransomware incident, minimizing data loss to an absolute minimum.

How to prevent having to use the Cybervault

No one ever wants to have to use the Cybervault. That is why I said it is the last-resort protection against malicious parties. We must prevent our IT systems from being abused, hijacked, or corrupted. In addition to creating immutable backups, we must take all necessary steps to prevent attackers from harming our systems. We see that access control is becoming increasingly tight. In addition, we need to take action to detect malicious access and behavior. This area is receiving increasing attention nowadays, and software tools and products to help with this task are becoming increasingly mature.

IBM Threat Detection for z/OS is one such new product. This tool helps detect and report anomalous and potentially malicious events on z/OS. The tool exploits AI technologies.

I believe this tool is only one of the functions we need to use to mitigate threats before they become a reality. AI technologies may help forecast malevolent activities before any harm can be done. It is not just an opportunity for software vendors. Generic solutions will help, but additional organization-specific features will also be required. Every organization has its own specific access patterns, data models, and change patterns, etcetera. Generic capabilities help, but only to a certain level. Organizations will also need to invest in solutions tailored to their specific needs and IT applications.

Cryptographic facilities on the mainframe

IBM Z mainframes are designed with extensive, built-in cryptographic capabilities that secure data and communications. These capabilities include specialized hardware to accelerate encryption and decryption, enabling the protection of large volumes of data with high performance. The z/OS operating system builds on this hardware foundation with integrated cryptographic services that support secure key management, encryption, digital signatures, and PIN processing for financial institutions, including support for quantum-safe encryption standards.

Integrated cryptographic facilities

The z/OS operating system includes the Integrated Cryptographic Service Facility (ICSF) as its core cryptographic subsystem. ICSF provides interfaces and services for managing and using cryptographic keys in conjunction with IBM Crypto Express hardware. It supports the generation, protection, and usage of symmetric and asymmetric keys, enabling secure encryption and decryption, digital signatures, and PIN processing.

ICSF is a fundamental component of z/OS security. It delivers the technical foundation for cryptographic operations, while governance, workflow, and auditing can be added through complementary solutions such as centralized key management facilities.

Key Management

Building on ICSF, many organizations require centralized management of cryptographic keys on z/OS. IBM provides the Enterprise Key Management Foundation (EKMF). EKMF manages the full lifecycle of cryptographic keys within the mainframe environment, adding workflows, auditing, and policy enforcement on top of ICSF.

EKMF is focused exclusively on the z/OS environment and IBM Z hardware. It enables organizations, especially in highly regulated industries such as banking and insurance, to implement a consistent, auditable, and compliant key management process for their mainframe workloads.

Many organizations are using comparable tools, including HSM-specific solutions such as Thales and nCipher, secrets management solutions such as CyberArk, or cloud-platform-specific solutions such as Google Cloud KMS or Azure Key Vault.

Pervasive encryption

Pervasive encryption is a relatively recent feature facilitated by the mainframe hardware. With pervasive encryption, data is always encrypted: data at rest is encrypted on disk, and internal connections between systems are encrypted in transit. Authorized users can only access this encrypted data with the correct decryption keys.

Pervasive encryption provides z/OS users with an additional layer of security. Even if a hacker gains access to the system and the files or datasets, the data remains unusable because it is encrypted. Similarly, even if communications between systems are intercepted, the data flowing over the network is always encrypted.

The final step is to encrypt all data in z/OS's working memory. Memory encryption is part of the architecture starting with the IBM z16 hardware model.

Mainframes and compliance

Mainframes have long served as the backbone of enterprise computing, particularly in industries like finance, healthcare, and government, where security, compliance, and data integrity are non-negotiable. The centralized architecture of the mainframe, with its dedicated security management, granular access controls, and unified policy enforcement, makes it uniquely capable of meeting stringent regulatory requirements, including GDPR, PCI-DSS, HIPAA, and SOX. This centralization not only provides organizations with greater control over their systems but also enables them to implement and manage that control more efficiently and effectively than distributed environments.

To further enhance these capabilities, vendors have developed specialized tools that integrate security and compliance management tasks directly into the mainframe environment. One tool I want to highlight briefly is IBM's Security and Compliance Center, which exemplifies the platform's strength in centralization.

This tool provides IT leaders with a streamlined, centralized approach to managing compliance across multiple regulations. By consolidating diverse compliance requirements into a single, cohesive framework, it eliminates the complexity of tracking each regulation manually. The Compliance Center also generates detailed reports and analytics, offering clear insights into compliance status and potential risks. This allows organizations to proactively address gaps and confidently demonstrate adherence during audits.

Chapter 13 System management for z/OS

The z/OS operating system is designed to host many applications on a single platform. From its beginning, efficient management of the applications and their underlying infrastructure has been an essential part of the z/OS ecosystem.

This chapter will discuss the regular system operations, monitoring processes, and tools you find on z/OS. I will also look at monitoring tools that ensure all our automated business, application, and technical processes are running as expected.

System operations

The z/OS operating system has an extensive operator interface that gives the system operator the tools to control the z/OS platform and its applications and intervene when issues occur. You can compare these operations facilities very well with the operations of physical processes, like in factories or power plants. The operator is equipped with many knobs, buttons, switches, and meters to keep the z/OS factory running.

Operator interfaces and some history

By design, the mainframe performs operations on so-called consoles. Consoles were originally physical terminal devices directly connected to the mainframe server via special equipment. Everything happening on the z/OS system was displayed on the console screens. A continuous newsfeed of messages generated by the numerous components running on the mainframe streamed over the console display. Warnings and failure messages were highlighted so an operator could quickly identify issues and take necessary actions.

Nowadays, physical consoles have been replaced by software equivalents. In the chapter on z/OS, I have already mentioned the IBM SDSF tool and similar tools from other vendors available on z/OS for this purpose. SDSF is the primary tool system operators and administrators use to view and manage the processes running on z/OS.

Additionally, z/OS has a central facility where information, warnings, and error messages from the hardware, operating system, middleware, and applications are gathered. This facility is called the system log and can be viewed in the SDSF tool.

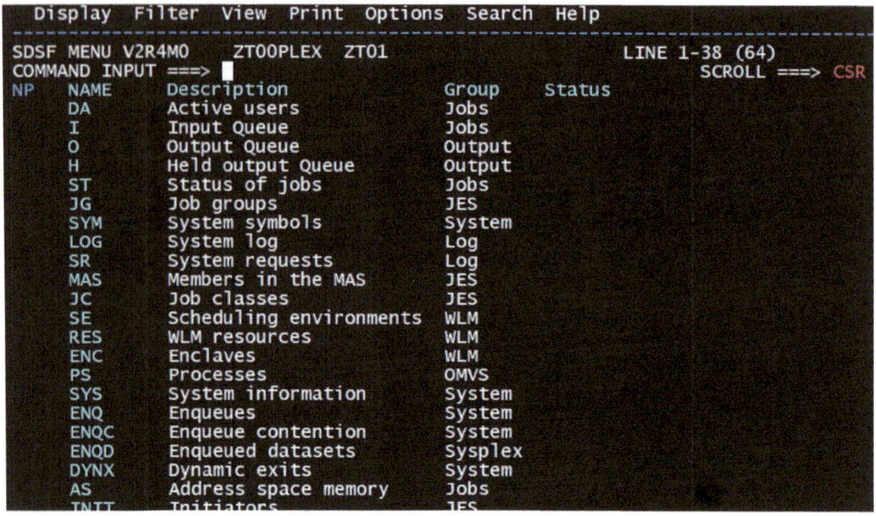

Figure 48 SDSF options

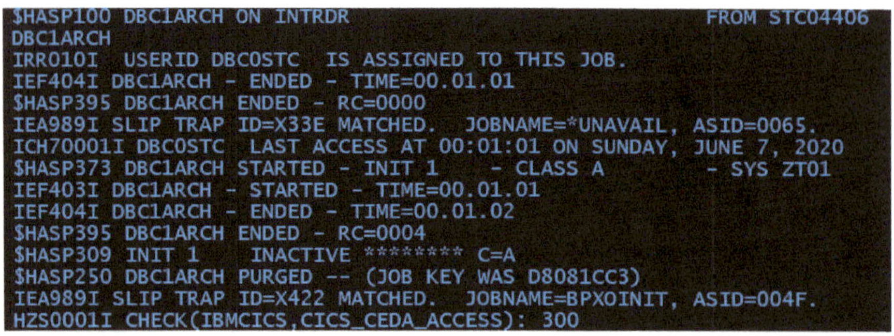

Figure 49 The system log viewed through SDSF

An operator can intervene with the running z/OS system and applications with operator commands. z/OS itself provides many of these operator commands for a wide variety of functions. The middleware tools installed on top of z/OS often also bring their own set of operator messages and commands.

Operator commands are like Unix commands for Unix operating systems, and functions provided by the Windows Task Manager and other Windows system administration functions. Operator commands can also be issued through application programming interfaces, which opens possibilities for building software to automate operations on the z/OS platform.

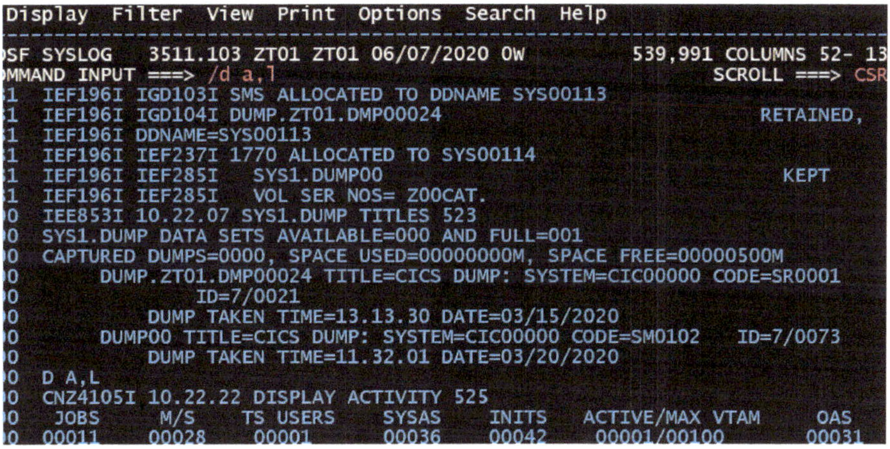

Figure 50 Executing an operator command through SDSF

Automated operations

In the past, a crew of operators managed the daily operations of the business processes running on a central computer, such as a mainframe. The operators were gathered in the control room, also called a bridge, from where they monitored and operated the processes running on the mainframe.

Nowadays, daily operations have been automated at most mainframe sites. All everyday issues are handled through automated processes, with special software overseeing these operations. Only in severe cases will the automation tools identify problems they cannot resolve, and an incident process will be initiated. A system or application administrator will then be called from their bed to investigate the issue.

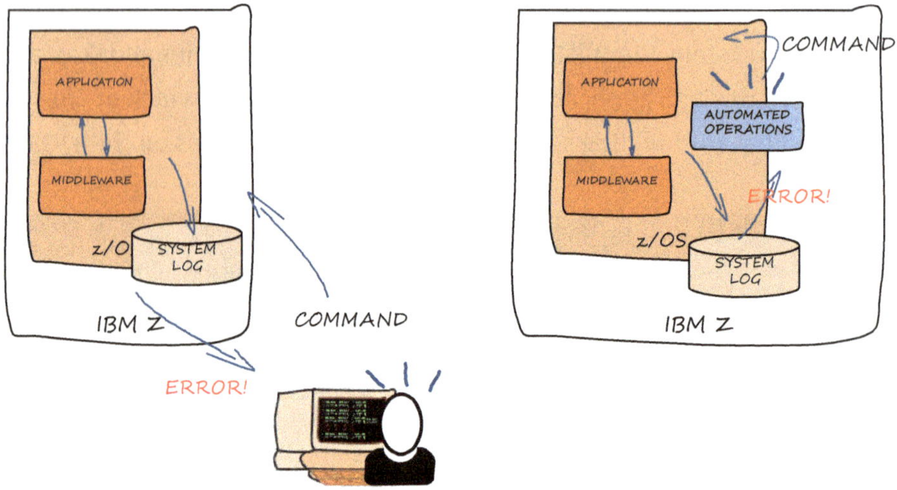

Figure 51 Manual versus automated operations

Several software suppliers provide automation tools for z/OS operations. All these tools monitor the messages flowing through the system log, which reports the health of everything running on z/OS. The occurrence of messages can be turned into events for which automated actions can be programmed.

For example, if z/OS signals that a pool of disk storage is filling up, the storage management software will write a message to the system log. An automation process that increases the storage pool and sends a notification email to the storage administrator can be defined. The automation process is kicked off automatically when the message appears in the system log.

All automated operations tools for z/OS are based on this mechanism. Some tools provide more help with automation tasks and advanced functions than others. Solutions in the market include System Automation from IBM, CA-OPS/MVS from Broadcom, and AUTOMON for z/OS from Macro4.

Monitoring

System management aims to ensure that all automated business processes run smoothly. For this, detailed information must be made available to assess the health of the running processes. All the z/OS and middleware components provide a wide variety of data that can be used to analyze the health of these individual components. The amount of data is so large that it is necessary to use tools that help make sense of all this data. This is where monitoring tools can help.

Monitoring tools apply to different levels of the operational system. In this section, I differentiate between infrastructure, application, and business monitoring for this chapter.

Figure 52 shows the different layers of monitoring that can be distinguished. It illustrates how application monitoring needs to be integrated to transform the information into meaningful business process monitoring.

The following sections will go into the different layers of monitoring in a bit more detail.

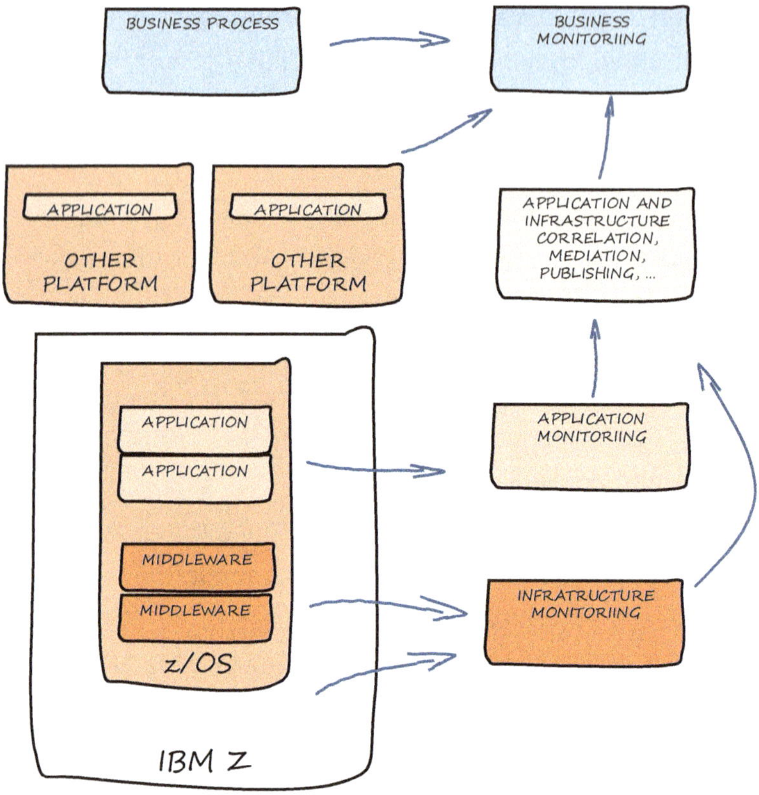

Figure 52 Monitoring of different business/IT layers

Infrastructure Monitoring for z/OS Environments

Infrastructure monitoring is critical for overseeing mainframe hardware, the z/OS operating system, and the middleware components running on it. These components generate extensive monitoring data, which is essential for assessing system health, performance, and operational efficiency.

z/OS includes built-in facilities for logging and monitoring data:

- System console messages are recorded in the system log for auditing and troubleshooting.

- The System Management Facility (SMF) provides a low-level interface, enabling infrastructure components to write detailed event records to SMF datasets for analysis.

However, while z/OS and its middleware produce abundant monitoring data, the challenge lies in extracting actionable insights from it. Traditional monitoring tools often focus on individual components, making it difficult to integrate data and achieve a holistic view of system health.

OpenTelemetry and Instrumented Middleware

Modern observability increasingly relies on OpenTelemetry, an open-standard framework for generating, collecting, and exporting telemetry data (metrics, logs, and traces). Instrumented middleware on z/OS, such as CICS, IMS, Db2, and MQ, can now produce OpenTelemetry-compatible data, enabling unified monitoring across hybrid environments. This allows organizations to correlate mainframe telemetry with data from distributed systems, providing a comprehensive, end-to-end view of performance and health.

Vendor Solutions for z/OS Monitoring

To address the need for meaningful monitoring, several vendors provide specialized tools for z/OS infrastructure:

- BMC's MainView monitors z/OS, CICS, IMS, Db2, and other critical components.
- IBM's Omegamon offers monitoring for z/OS, storage, networks, and middleware like CICS, IMS, and Db2.
- ASG-TMON provides a suite of tools for monitoring z/OS infrastructure and middleware.
- Broadcom's Intelligent Operations and Automation includes tools for z/OS and network monitoring.

While these solutions help organizations leverage monitoring data, integrating them into a unified observability strategy, especially with OpenTelemetry, remains a key challenge for modern mainframe environments.

Application monitoring

The next level of monitoring provides a view of the applications' and their components' functioning.

Off-the-shelf tools or frameworks do not provide comprehensive support for this monitoring level for application in COBOL or PL/I. Application monitoring and logging frameworks such as Java Management Extensions and Log4J are available for Java, but similar tools are not available for languages like COBOL and PL/I. Many z/OS users have developed application-monitoring frameworks, relying on various technologies.

Some tools can provide a certain level of application monitoring. For example, Dynatrace, AppDynamics, and IBM Application Performance Management provide capabilities to examine application behavior. However, the functionality is often not easily extensible for application developers, as with the log4j and JMX mentioned above. There remains a need for a framework (preferably open-source) that allows application developers to create specific monitoring and logging information and events at particular points within an application on z/OS.

Business Monitoring: Bridging IT and Business Outcomes

Business-level monitoring remains one of the most complex challenges in IT. Despite decades of advancements, there is still no unified standard or approach for monitoring end-to-end business processes. While technical monitoring is mature, aligning it with business objectives—such as customer experience, operational efficiency, and revenue impact—requires deeper integration and contextual understanding.

OpenTelemetry Standardizes observability

OpenTelemetry has become the industry-standard framework for application instrumentation, providing a vendor-neutral way to collect, process, and export telemetry data—including metrics, logs, and traces—across all languages and platforms. By standardizing data generation and transmission, OpenTelemetry simplifies integration with diverse observability tools.

Its true value lies in its ability to aggregate and enrich data from multiple sources, offering a holistic view of the IT infrastructure that supports critical business processes. This enables organizations to correlate technical performance with business outcomes, such as transaction success rates, service-level agreements (SLAs), and customer satisfaction.

z/OS Monitoring Integration

Recent advancements have enabled seamless integration of z/OS monitoring data into modern observability platforms. Tools like Syncsort's IronStream and IBM's Common Data Provider collect data from system logs, application logs, and SMF records, forwarding it to centralized platforms such as Splunk, Elastic, or Grafana.

This integration breaks down silos between mainframe and distributed systems, enabling cross-platform visibility (as shown in Figure 52 Monitoring of different business/IT layersFigure 52). By consolidating mainframe data with other IT telemetry, organizations achieve a unified view of their entire infrastructure, bridging legacy and modern environments to support business continuity and performance.

Modern Observability Platforms

Today's observability platforms, such as Splunk, Elastic, Prometheus, and Grafana, go beyond traditional monitoring. They provide:

- Sophisticated data aggregation for real-time insights.

- Advanced analysis to detect anomalies before they impact operations.
- Visualization capabilities to correlate events across hybrid environments and identify root causes.
- Performance trend tracking aligned with business KPIs.

By leveraging these platforms, organizations can transform raw telemetry data into actionable insights, ensuring IT monitoring directly supports business goals, whether it's maintaining uptime, optimizing costs, or enhancing customer experiences.

The Business Value of Observability

This approach ensures that technical monitoring is not just about tracking system health but is aligned with business value. By integrating OpenTelemetry, z/OS data streams, and modern observability platforms, organizations can:

- Proactively address issues before they impact customers or revenue.
- Optimize IT operations to enhance business agility.
- Make data-driven decisions that improve both technical performance and business outcomes.

Ultimately, the goal is to monitor systems not just for their technical state, but for their impact on the business, ensuring continuity, performance, and competitive advantage.

Chapter 14 Modern mainframe application architectures

This chapter aims to provide an overview of the main principles and building blocks of the architecture of modern applications on a mainframe. First, I will discuss what a traditional mainframe application looks like. Next, I will present a contemporary approach to architecting mainframe applications.

Main characteristics and principles

Well-designed mainframe applications have always featured distinct layers for presentation functions, business logic, and data logic. This general application architecture best practice has been in place for decades. When web development emerged, this concept was reinvented and given a fancier name: the Model-View-Controller (MVC) paradigm.

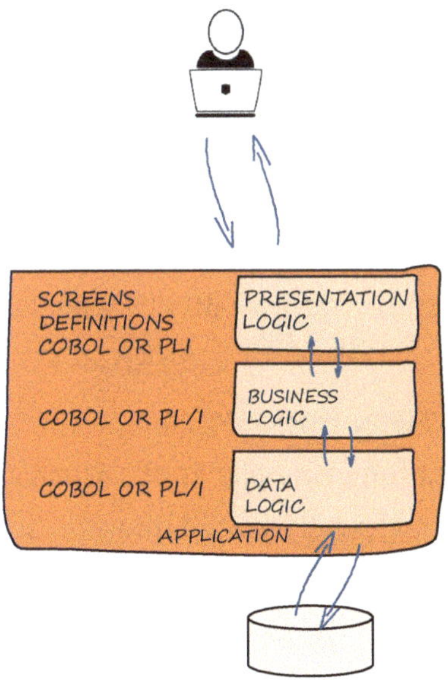

Figure 53 A neatly layered traditional mainframe application

With the advent of service-oriented architectures and web technologies, application and enterprise architecture approaches have evolved. A different approach to separating duties and positioning technologies emerged to build modern application landscapes, fundamentally changing how we should position and build z/OS applications today.

Architecture principles

Several architectural principles determine today's best practice mainframe architecture.

Layers of applications

The first principle is the enterprise architecture principle of cleanly separating functional high layers in the enterprise-level architecture. These layers often include a front-office or channel layer, a mid-office or integration layer, and a back-office layer. Depending on your organization, more layers may be applicable to ensure a clean separation of duties and maintainability of the software we build.

Layers within applications

The second principle is to separate applications internally into layers, typically in a presentation, business logic, and data access layers.

Applications own their data (data belongs to an application)

The third principle is that an application is responsible for its data. Or, to phrase it differently, all data belongs to one application. This principle reemerged with the microservices architecture, but was already a best practice long before.

Communication between layers is service-oriented

The fourth principle is the service orientation principle: applications can only access each other's logic and data through well-defined and exposed service interfaces. This means one application must not directly access data from another application.

Case Study: The cost of ignoring Service-Oriented Architecture (SOA) principles

At an insurance company, the lack of service-oriented architecture (SOA) principles resulted in significant technical debt. Historically, premium calculations were handled exclusively by intermediaries, who used a dedicated mainframe company application to perform these tasks for their customers.

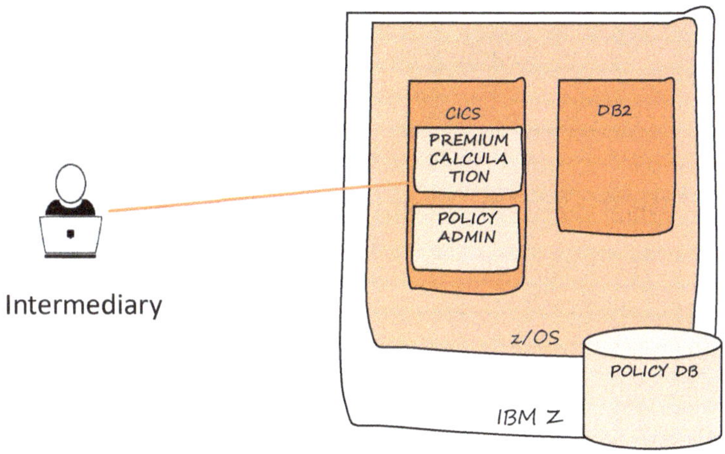

Figure 54 A tightly coupled insurance application

When the company decided to transition to a self-service model, allowing customers to calculate their own premiums, they encountered a significant obstacle: the premium calculation logic was deeply entangled in the presentation layer, the front-end processes of their mainframe application. This tight coupling made it difficult to expose the functionality directly to customers via an internet-enabled platform.

To enable self-service, the company had to disentangle the premium calculation logic from the monolithic front-end, a complex and resource-intensive effort. This challenge could have been avoided by adhering to long-established mainframe best practices, such as modular design and separation of concerns.

Ultimately, the company succeeded in refactoring the application, resulting in a more flexible, future-proof architecture (as illustrated in Figure 56). This experience underscores the importance of SOA principles in ensuring scalability and adaptability, even in legacy systems.

Position of the mainframe in modern application landscapes

In today's architecture continuum, mainframe applications typically operate in the back-office layer. Some mid-office applications may exist on the mainframe, but you rarely find front-office applications on z/OS. Applications on z/OS are good at running high volumes of transactions, involving large amounts of updates in a database and other resources, and possibly combining this with an analytical capability in these databases using the IDAA facility (see section Special topic: IBM Db2 Analytics Accelerator (IDAA): Boosting Mainframe Analytics) and Artificial Intelligence technology.

Therefore, modern mainframe applications rarely have presentation logic. The only presentation logic needed on z/OS may be to manage the IT applications themselves. Modern z/OS applications are headless and comprise integration, business, and data logic.

The integration logic handles interface specifics. This layer shields the technical interface details from the business logic, allowing a single piece of business logic to be reused across multiple service interfaces.

The business logic in the mainframe applications is exposed to other applications through standardized service interfaces. These services are consumed by frontend applications or by a mid-tier layer that orchestrates multiple services (APIs) into business functions.

Mid-tier functions here include partner services exposed through an API portal to 3rd parties that build applications on top of the (mainframe and other) service APIs.

So, how will this hang together? Omitting details that would make many architects go crazy, a reference architecture for mainframe applications and integration in an enterprise context is shown in Figure 55.

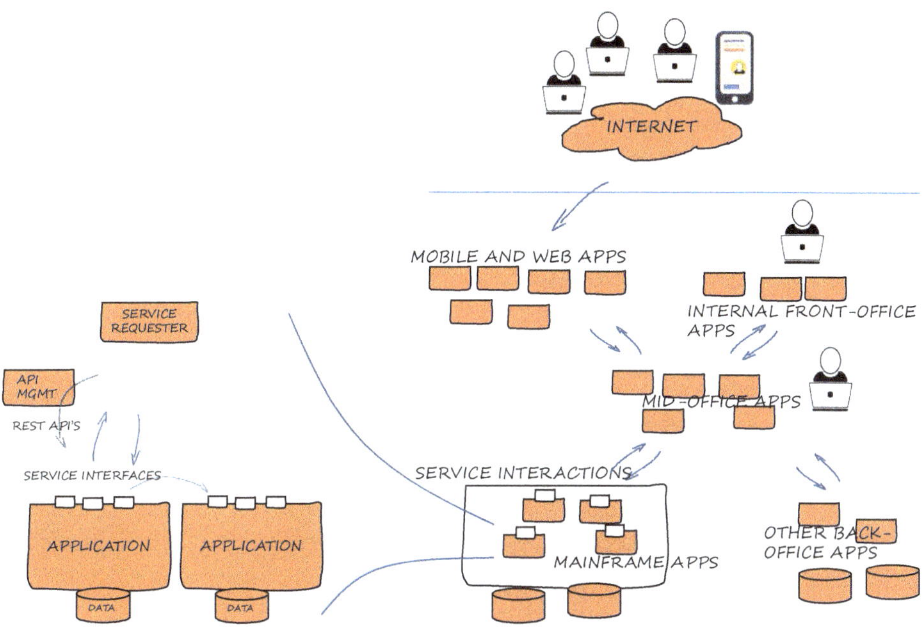

Figure 55 Mainframe applications in a modern IT landscape

The main characteristics of a z/OS application

In the architectural context described, a modern mainframe application exhibits the following key characteristics:

- Presentation Logic Separation. Modern mainframe applications typically do not include presentation logic. If a presentation layer exists on the mainframe, it serves solely as a management interface for mainframe applications, usually a web-based interface rather than a legacy 3270 green screen.
- No Business Presentation Layers. Business applications on the mainframe do not include end-user presentation interfaces. Instead, they focus on backend processing and expose functionality through standardized interfaces.
- Layered Architecture Internally, applications are structured into logical layers, including:
    - Service interface handlers (external interactions)
    - Business logic (core application functionality)
    - Data logic (data access and processing)
- Service-Oriented Design. Applications are service-oriented, exposing well-defined services to other applications and internal components. This design ensures modularity and reusability.
- Controlled Data Access. Applications only access data from other applications through services, never directly. This means no direct access to files or databases owned by another application, ensuring data encapsulation and security.

Service Interfaces: Beyond REST APIs

A common misconception is that service interfaces must be web services or REST APIs. In reality, they can also include:

- Message-queueing interfaces (e.g., IBM MQ)
- File-based interfaces (e.g., data exchange via files)
- Native call interfaces (e.g., direct program-to-program calls within z/OS)

For applications running on z/OS, native call interfaces can optimize performance for co-located applications while maintaining functional decoupling. While some may argue against this approach, pragmatic optimization, rather than rigid adherence to a single paradigm, is key. The critical principle is that components interact through well-defined interfaces, abstracting implementation details from one another.

Case study: Creating a modern application and integration architecture with mainframe applications

Figure 56 illustrates a simplified real-world architecture (from the insurance company case study I mentioned in the Architecture principles section earlier in this book) that showcases a z/OS backend integrated with modern service interfaces.

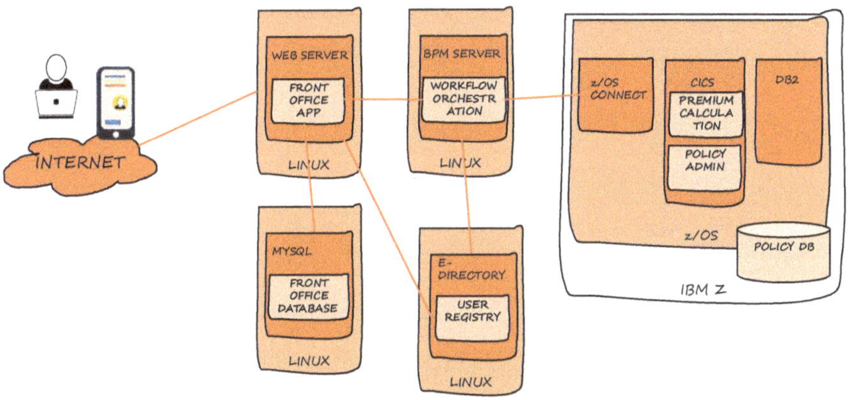

Figure 56 Example architecture overview with z/OS backend

Bridging the Gap: From Ideal to Reality

In this chapter, I have outlined the architecture of a modern mainframe application, presenting an idealized vision of how applications should be designed. However, the reality is far more complex. Many mainframe environments are burdened by decades of legacy systems, outdated practices, and accumulated technical debt.

In the Transformation strategies chapter, I will explore this legacy of technical debt, examining its origins and impact. Most importantly, I will discuss practical strategies to eliminate it. The goal is to transform outdated systems into agile, maintainable, and future-proof applications while preserving the reliability for which mainframes are known.

But first, we need to address the inevitable question that underlies every mainframe discussion: cost.

Chapter 15 Understanding mainframe cost

Let's address the elephant in the room: cost. The financial commitment tied to mainframe computing is often the foremost concern for both current users and organizations considering mainframe investments. Yet all too often, there is no complete understanding of what truly drives these costs.

This chapter offers a transparent breakdown of the mainframe's total cost of ownership. I'll show you where the money goes, why costs seem high, and, most importantly, where you have control. By the end, you'll understand mainframe economics not as a mystery, but as a manageable business decision. At the end, I hope you will be able to assess mainframe economics not just in terms of upfront costs, but in the context of enterprise-scale computing needs and long-term business objectives.

An overview of the cost of a mainframe

Mainframe costs fall into three categories: hardware, software, and management.

- Management costs are installing, maintaining, and operating the hardware and software in a mainframe configuration.
- Hardware costs include acquiring and maintaining the mainframe server machines, storage devices, and other necessary equipment.
- Software costs are the licenses and maintenance fees paid for the required software components.

The most significant cost component of a mainframe setup is software. I estimate, albeit unscientifically, that two-thirds of the total mainframe costs are attributable to software. Hardware and management each account for half of the remaining costs, so each is approximately one-sixth of the total.

The cost of managing a mainframe configuration

The costs of managing the mainframe primarily consist of personnel expenses. I will describe what kind of people you need and elaborate on the associated costs for these roles.

Who do you need to run a mainframe?

To run a mainframe computer requires several roles. Roles are often combined into a single person or into one or more persons in small mainframe shops. In larger mainframe setups, you will find that roles are even more specialized. The terminology I use below is mine. Role names may vary across organizations, but the responsibilities remain the same everywhere.

- Engineering. The engineering team installs and configures mainframe hardware, the operating system, and middleware software components.
- Operations. A centralized operations team ensures the daily operation and functioning of the mainframe's central components.
- Application management. The application management team manages the daily functioning of one or more applications running on the mainframe. They perform this task as part of the application's business process. In a modern DevOps organization, these teams perform the Ops side of a DevOps team.
- Application development. The application development team analyzes, develops, and tests new application functionality. They perform the Dev side of a DevOps team.
- Security management. This special role authorizes the mainframe management staff, end users, and application functions to perform the necessary processes.
- Database management. Because the mainframe's database systems are shared, database management is often centralized. DBAs

perform database management tasks for multiple application teams on the mainframe platforms.

- Batch planning. Many organizations rely on a complex batch-processing schedule. They often manage batch-planning tools centrally to optimize scheduling and meet overall timelines.
- Storage management. A mainframe storage management team oversees disk and tape resources, monitoring utilization, performing capacity planning, and ensuring reliable storage availability.

Thus, the management cost of a mainframe platform largely depends on your organization's setup and the investments you have made in automating repetitive tasks.

The benefits of centralized management

Most of the mainframe's features are shared, and its management is centralized. Operating the mainframe platform is relatively efficient compared to similar distributed and cloud platforms.

Nowadays, most, if not all, of the daily operations of a modern mainframe platform and the management of its applications are automated. In the past, a group of physical operators managed the mainframe, gathered in an operations room. Nowadays, specialized automation software enables automation of daily tasks, and operating rooms have largely become obsolete.

In summary, the management cost of a mainframe platform depends largely on your organization's setup and the investments you have made in automating repetitive management tasks.

The cost of hardware for the mainframe

In this section, I will outline the components of the mainframe hardware and their cost structure. For now, it is enough to know that for a mainframe environment, you need the following categories:

- A capacity entitlement.
- The mainframe server machine(s).
- The devices for storing data.
- The components connect the mainframe servers and storage devices and connect them to the rest of the data center.
- Hardware maintenance.

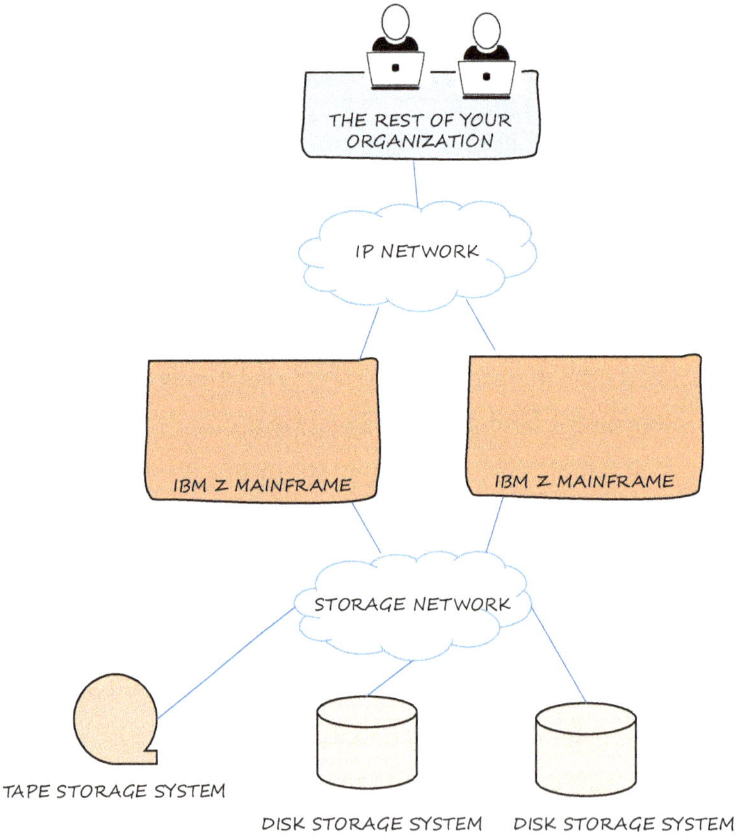

Figure 57 A typical mainframe hardware setup

The capacity entitlement

First, we need to look at a quirky aspect. When you buy a new mainframe server as a first-time user, you pay for two parts: the new physical machine(s) and a capacity entitlement. The physical machine is obvious and comprises all the materials you purchase and install in a data center. We will look at that in the next section.

The second part, the capacity entitlement, is a virtual unit that specifies how much of the physical machine you can utilize. A physical machine can provide significantly more capacity than you need and are entitled to. In the microcode, an IBM engineer will configure how much of the server you can access and impose limitations on that. You buy an entitlement once.

When you acquire a new machine to replace an older model, you should only need to purchase the new physical hardware. IBM calls this the carry-forward principle: your entitlements move with your hardware. Thus, if you are regularly buying new hardware, you may skip capacity entitlement upgrades. However, if you do not follow the hardware generations, you could lose your capacity entitlements.

From an accounting standpoint, you have the costs of the physical parts, which depreciate over a preferred number of years. Additionally, you periodically pay for maintenance and support of the equipment. The quirky capacity entitlement is a bookkeeping unit that you pay for once and record in the books as an intangible asset.

Mainframe server machines

Several factors determine the costs of a mainframe server: CPU capacity, memory, and other server components.

CPU capacity

When purchasing a mainframe, you must first assess the CPU capacity required. The CPU capacity significantly influences the machine's cost and, as we have noted, the software price. You can acquire CPU capacity at a very granular level.

When you buy a laptop or an Intel server, you choose a particular CPU type, for which you have a few choices, and the number of CPUs you need. When you buy a mainframe server, you have a variety of choices for the number of CPUs you need and a wide variety of choices for the capacity of these CPUs. A mainframe server has hundreds of CPU capacity options. Your technical staff can tell which of these hundreds of options would be best through precise measurements. IBM provides tools to help you determine this.

You might wonder how IBM accomplishes this. Do they create hundreds of variations of CPUs? No, they do not. Instead, through a mechanism called microcode, IBM can program its single generic CPU in such a way that it delivers a specific amount of CPU power. With each new machine, IBM publishes a detailed table of all the possible CPU capacity options. See (IBM Z Large Systems Performance Reference, 2025).

Now, the question is, why does IBM do this? What is so tricky about the CPU capacity of a mainframe server? As we saw in the previous section on software costs, the CPU capacity of the mainframe server directly affects the software costs. A slight increase in CPU capacity often significantly impacts these costs. That is also why I mentioned at the beginning of this chapter that the most significant part of your mainframe costs will be software. So, IBM does this to give you small increments in mainframe computing capacity.

It is essential to note that each mainframe server model provides a comprehensive range of CPU capacity options. You need help from a specialist to determine which model is right for you.

Memory

A mainframe server can have a lot of memory. Calculating the amount of memory you need is relatively straightforward. Memory for a mainframe used to be very expensive, but it is relatively cheap nowadays. Modern applications assume you have a lot of memory, so buy enough. There is no reason to be frugal with memory when purchasing mainframe hardware. Not anymore.

Other server components

Other components that determine a mainframe server's cost include networking cards, I/O cards, cryptographic and compression cards, the new AI acceleration cards, and more. Although the cost of these components is not negligible, it is straightforward to determine what you need from them.

Mainframe storage costs

Storage systems are special devices that provide storage for a mainframe server. These systems connect to the mainframe server over unique fiber connections.

For your mainframe, you need one or more storage systems and fiber-optic devices to connect your storage systems to your mainframe server or servers.

Storage systems come in different flavors. First, there is *disk storage,* which can vary in amount and type. Data can still be stored on spinning disks, flash drives, or a combination of both. Spinning disks are cheaper but slower, and are hardly used in modern storage systems.

The second storage flavor is *tape storage.* A tape storage system comprises tape units, tape readers, and, optionally, a tape library. A tape library is a device that stores your tape cartridges. The tape library will automatically store and retrieve them. Sometimes, this device is referred to as a tape robot because it features a robot-like mechanism within the tape library. The robot transports the tape cartridges from the tape drive to the safe and back. The price of tape solutions is determined by the number of units required, the type of tape, and the complexity of the tape library device.

The cost of Mainframe connectivity devices

To connect your mainframe to your organization's network and data center(s), you need additional equipment: networking cards in the server, fiber optic or copper cables, network switches, extenders, and possibly network routers.

If you have multiple mainframe servers, you may also need specialized fiber-optic cables and devices to interconnect them and enable fast communication.

Hardware maintenance

For all hardware components, it is common to include a maintenance agreement. The supplier ensures the timely repair or replacement of defective components to minimize downtime. The agreement typically specifies response times, service levels, and cost coverage. This ensures reliable system performance and predictable maintenance expenses.

Why is mainframe hardware so expensive, and why not

The mainframe components are more expensive than what you are used to paying for similar computing equipment for other servers. Why is that? I will explain. However, I will also put these high costs in context.

It's expensive, for good and not-so-good reasons

The main factors leading to high mainframe server costs are:

- High manufacturing costs,
- The mainframe's redundant design comes at a cost, and
- The monopoly position of IBM in the mainframe server space.

The first factor leading to the high cost of servers is the cost of manufacturing a mainframe. Since the number of mainframes built each year is relatively small, hardware design and manufacturing can only partially benefit from economies of scale.

The design and manufacturing process for mainframes is subject to extensive quality controls, an extremely rigorous approach to building reliability into mainframes that results in higher manufacturing costs. The upside is, of course, that you get a piece of hardware that is more robust and thus has better availability than commodity server hardware.

Furthermore, all parts in the mainframe box are configured redundantly, meaning the machine has at least two instances of each component. This redundancy ensures that the failure of any single element cannot bring down the whole box, but it comes at additional cost.

The final reason for the high price of mainframe hardware is that IBM is the only manufacturer. Amdahl was the last competitor to withdraw from manufacturing IBM mainframe-compatible servers. There is no competition, and their mainframe clients cannot purchase mainframe hardware elsewhere.

These three factors are real and significant. But the story doesn't end there. When you evaluate hardware costs in the context of what you're replacing and the total cost of achieving equivalent capability, the picture changes significantly.

The mainframe is not as expensive as it seems

A mainframe is expensive, but some aspects put this high price into perspective.

If you look more closely at the hardware architecture and compare a mainframe to a commodity x86 server, it is an apples-to-oranges comparison. In a mainframe, you get a lot of computing facilities integrated into a single box. All these facilities should be compared with a stack of x86 servers wired with connectivity equipment. To make a fair comparison between the two, you should not just compare the servers but also consider *connectivity needs and management costs*.

Further, when assessing processing capacity, some specific technical factors should also be considered. In the mainframe box, you get extra computing capacity in the *dedicated I/O processing* unit, called the I/O subsystem, and special processor(s) for compression, encryption, and other functions. On x86 hardware, you usually run these functions on your standard CPUs. Therefore, you would again need more or larger x86 servers to achieve similar processing power.

We have seen that all mainframe components are redundantly engineered. To achieve a similar *redundancy* with x86 servers, you must include additional x86 servers and connectivity components in your comparison.

You will stack many *more application environments* on a single mainframe than you would on x86 servers. You will run all your Development, Test, Acceptance, and Production environments on one or a few mainframe servers. For a comparable configuration for all these environments, you will need many more x86 servers.

Finally, a mainframe configuration with fewer servers and peripherals requires fewer *data center facilities*: less floor space, cooling, and electricity. This also reduces the relative cost of mainframes.

In summary, a mainframe hardware configuration is a straightforward setup of one or two boxes connected to your network infrastructure via a small number of network connections. A comparable x86 infrastructure will require a significantly larger number of x86 servers and additional switches, routers, cabling, and patching, resulting in higher management costs and increased data center facility expenses.

The cost of mainframe software

In the following section, I will explain how the software costs for the mainframe are structured. Be warned: this is a complex topic. I will describe software license models and discuss the main calculation concepts underpinning them.

Understanding the cost of software on z/OS: MLC, and OTC

There are two main types of software licenses available for the mainframe. The first is MLC, which stands for Monthly License Charge. With MLC, you pay a monthly fee for the use of the software. The monthly amount is based on how much you have used. I will explain this amount in more detail later.

The second type of software license is OTC, which stands for One-Time Charge. With OTC licensing, you pay once for a perpetual entitlement to use a piece of software.

Below, I will elaborate on both MLC and OTC.

The MLC license model

Traditionally, z/OS software is "paid per use" under the MLC license model. With MLC, you pay a variable monthly sum to your software supplier(s). This sum is calculated based on the peak CPU capacity you used that month. The amount of CPU you use is measured in units called MSUs, which stand for *Million Service Units.*

The monthly peak in CPU usage is calculated over a four-hour period. The determining number over those four hours is the "four-hour rolling average," also known as 4HRA. The *peak 4HRA* for a month is the MSU number during the four-hour period in that month during which you used the most CPU.

Understanding the 4HRA is critical. Your workloads can peak as high as needed, but your software bill is unaffected if they do not influence the

4HRA peak. Figure 58 illustrates how you can have very high peak capacity usage without affecting the 4HRA peak.

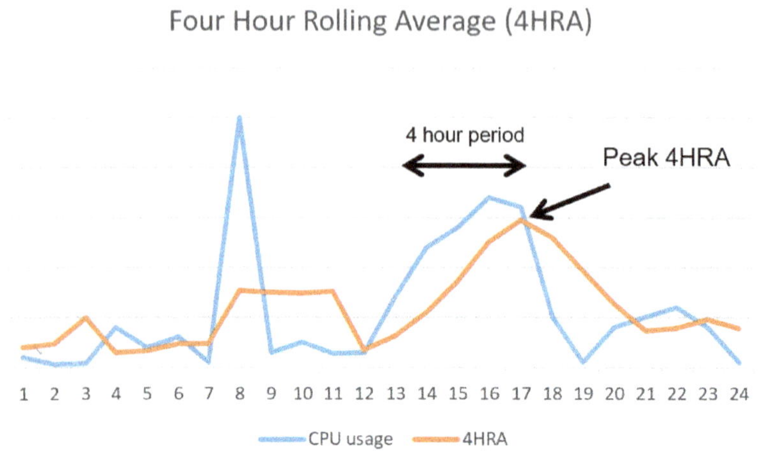

Figure 58 Peak four-hour rolling average (4HRA)

The OTC license model

A more recent license model on z/OS is a perpetual license model, also used for software on other platforms. This model is called OTC, which stands for One-Time Charge (as opposed to the recurring charge with MLC). OTC is available for a selected number of z/OS software components.

With the OTC model, you purchase an entitlement to use a software product for a specific, agreed-upon maximum computing capacity. The entitlement is limited to a *maximum* capacity. Therefore, this does not have the flexibility to calculate *used* capacity, as in the MLC model.

The OTC license model is often based on the same 4HRA formula as the MLC software. Some license models may use other metrics, like the number of instances, the number of transactions processed, or the amount of data stored. You must buy additional license entitlements when you exceed the metric, be it capacity, instances, or other units to which you are entitled.

As with regular perpetual license models, for OTC software you can optionally purchase subscription and support services. The fee is typically calculated as a percentage of the original license acquisition cost, usually around 20%. By subscribing to these services, you gain access to software upgrades and technical support. This support allows you to contact the software vendor for assistance with software issues, including emergencies, and for technical questions related to the product, ensuring smooth operation and access to the latest features.

Other license models

Nowadays, several additional license models are primarily variations of the OTC or MLC. I will highlight these later in the "New license models and their limitations" section, but let's first examine the issues with traditional MLC license terms.

For open-source software, the typical model involves obtaining support through a standard open-source support agreement, which provides assistance for the open-source software you deploy.

Clearing up MSU smoke and mirrors

I mentioned the mysterious abbreviation MSU above as the metric for computing capacity (CPU volume) in software usage and licensing bills. Understanding MSU is critical to understanding your software bill, the largest component of your mainframe budget.

This section is somewhat technical, but necessary. MSU is used in various contexts, including mainframe hardware capacity calculations, software charging, and capacity and performance contexts.

Many mainframe users get that glazed look in their eyes when MSUs come up. Many mainframe specialists get that glazed look, unless they are experts in capacity and performance management or salespeople. And even then.

I will try to clear up the muddy waters of MSUs here.

MSU is a capacity unit

MSU is a unit of computing capacity.

That's it.

Unfortunately, MSU is a somewhat abstract concept, and it has a complex relationship with real-world phenomena.

First, the basics.

MSU stands for *Millions of Service Units*. A *Service Unit* (SU) is a concept for computing capacity on the mainframe. You can compare it to kWh or (Millions of) Instructions per Second – *MIPS*, a comparable term for other computer systems.

With MIPS, the manufacturer determines a computer's capacity by counting the number of CPU instructions it can process per second.

The calculation for service units is a bit more complicated. A Service Unit is calculated by IBM by averaging the possible instructions of a mainframe server and counting the number that can be processed within a specific period. Some instructions are simple and can be executed quickly, while others are more complex. Thus, the service unit calculation considers how often and how complex specific CPU instructions are used.

The MSU capacity indicates the number of Service Units a mainframe computer can process per hour.

That could be all of it, but we are still not there. Unfortunately, one MSU is not the same as another. There are hardware MSUs and software MSUs, with subtle but significant differences between them.

Hardware and software MSUs

It is essential to understand the difference between hardware and software MSUs when calculating the mainframe's cost.

The hardware MSU number is the mainframe box's capacity as it rolls off the factory floor. IBM has calculated it for a specific combination of hardware components, and that's it. The hardware MSU number determines (amongst other things) the cost of your mainframe server machine.

However, this hardware MSU number is not the MSU number used to calculate your software bill. IBM uses the *software MSU* number for this purpose. The hardware MSU number of the configuration serves as the basis to calculate the software MSU number.

For each new hardware generation, the ratio of hardware to software MSUs is set. IBM originally invented the software MSU concept to provide a discount on the software bill when customers migrated to newer hardware. So if you got a 10% discount on the software bill, after four consecutive hardware generations, each offering the same discount, the cumulative ratio between hardware and software MSU numbers reached 0,9^4 = 0,6561. This is no longer done. IBM has developed other methods to reduce the software bill by introducing further discounts for customers running on the latest hardware generations. This incentivizes the mainframe user to buy new hardware, and the software cost reduction on the latest hardware can offset the investment.

Now, if we look at the software costs on the mainframe, it is the monthly number of *software MSUs* in your peak four-hour rolling average that determines the total amount you owe the software vendor under mainframe license models.

Vendors also offer Flex Capacity models, which provide additional flexibility in how software costs are calculated. Some software can be billed based on total MSU hours consumed per month, a pay-per-use model where a baseline or minimum usage is established. Usage above this baseline incurs additional charges, allowing organizations to align costs more closely with actual consumption. Alternatively, full-capacity models allow organizations to use the entire available capacity of their mainframe for a fixed cost, providing predictable billing and avoiding unexpected cost fluctuations.

> In short: MSU measures how much computing power your mainframe uses, and it directly impacts your software costs. Work with your vendor to optimize this. If you lack experience in this area, consider engaging an experienced consultant to guide you.

How unique is this MSU abracadabra to the mainframe?

Is this complex abracadabra so different and specific for the mainframe?

Yes and No. Yes, the confusing terminology of MLC, MSU, and 4HRA is unique, as is the complexity and granularity of the MSU calculation.

And no. Relative capacity numbers are also used on other computing hardware. Vendors like Microsoft, SAP, Oracle, and IBM assign arbitrary values to different CPU types to calculate license costs for running software on those CPUs. And through this arbitrariness, they can steer the software bill they will send you as their customer.

Finally, MSUs for peak workloads – don't let that confuse you (it will anyway)

Your performance engineer may one day say, "We need 100 MSUs to handle our peak of 1,000 transactions per second on our busiest business day."

How should you respond to that? You read the paragraphs above, and now you think: wasn't MSU a capacity number *per hour*? How does that relate to the capacity needed for a peak workload measured *per second*?

In a way, indeed, it doesn't. As we have seen in the previous section, MSUs express the capacity of a mainframe configuration in Service Units per hour.

Your performance engineer means he needs a configuration—an LPAR or a set of LPARs—with a total capacity of 100 MSUs. In other words, a machine can process 100 MSUs in one hour. We need that capacity only to run the workload with the right performance during the peak period, which is often much shorter than an hour. This peak does not necessarily impact the monthly 4HRA. Your software bill will not be based on the 100 MSUs that your performance specialist mentioned. This peak may not impact your four-hour rolling average at all.

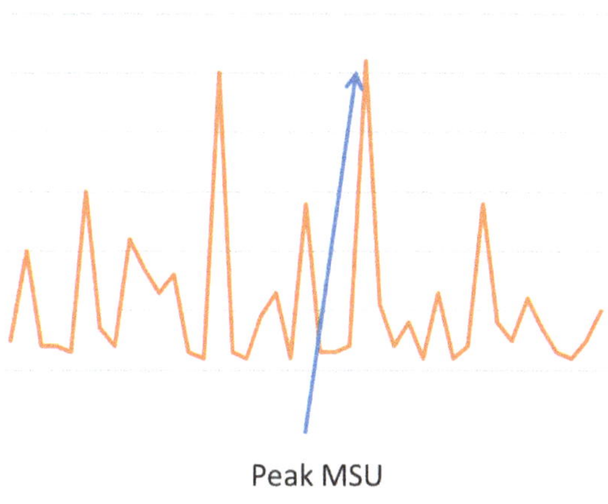

Figure 59 Peak MSU

So, the best response by far to your performance and capacity engineer's capacity estimate would be: 'Do you mean Software MSUs or Hardware MSUs?' And you will be best friends forever after.

Special topics related to mainframe costs

In the previous sections, I have explained the parts that contribute to the total cost of your mainframe platform.

In this section, I will discuss a few other interesting topics related to mainframe costs.

New License Models: Opportunities and Pitfalls

You might wonder why IBM and other mainframe software vendors continue to use this complex and unattractive MSU-based model. The complex cost model is putting off customers from the mainframe platform, and the vendors are very aware of this. A Catch-22?

The reason is straightforward: the vendors wish to protect their current income stream. Suppose they change the financial model for their customers' existing workloads. In that case, that will directly impact these vendors' income streams and, thus, their bottom-line business results, even if this is short-term and detrimental to their longer-term financial health.

There are many different new license models

Fortunately, many mainframe software vendors have created new software licensing models to make running new workloads on the mainframe affordable and competitive with other computing platforms.

There are many new software license models available nowadays, including variations of the MLC model, some based on the OTC model, and others that are even more flexible and creative. You can easily count twenty different license models on mainframe software vendors' websites.

As a mainframe user, it is therefore essential to know that when you have a new workload, you negotiate different terms for running it. Do not extrapolate existing cost models to new workloads. Discuss with your vendors the best new license model applicable to the new situation.

Benefits and pitfalls of new license models

It is impossible to discuss the details of all these license models here. I encourage you to discuss these options with your suppliers; even more creative options may be available. However, it would be helpful to consider a few key points when purchasing software for the mainframe.

First, the new license models are designed to offer greater flexibility. In other words, commercially, anything is possible. Your imagination and your software vendor are the only limitations. When you are in a situation where you are building a new application on the mainframe or expanding existing workloads, your software suppliers will help you with new, more flexible licensing solutions to make this possible. It is not unusual to discuss this directly with your software vendor's executives before detailing the software deal with the sales and procurement teams.

But be aware, there are pitfalls. The new license models may, by default, require some form of technical constraint to make it easy to measure the new workload for billing purposes, thereby retaining existing workload measurements. The technical limitations can make your configuration operationally (a lot) less efficient. For example, some license models require the new workloads to run in separate LPARs. Such a setup may facilitate the measurement of license usage, but from a technical perspective, it may have a significant impact on the efficiency of your z/OS operations. Therefore, you should have a good understanding of the technological consequences of such constraints. Include your technical staff in the licensing discussions since they can assess the impact of the limitations imposed by the licensing model.

In general, the license model must never compromise the best technical solution. My experience is that transparent collaboration with your vendors will provide an optimal solution.

Super-expensive software vendors

You may find that your organization is paying unsustainable costs for mainframe tools while receiving minimal value from these tools and from supplier support. These vendors often operate on a cash cow business model, prioritizing revenue extraction over customer satisfaction and product improvement.

The most effective solution is to plan for migration away from these high-cost tools aggressively. Alternative software exists for virtually all mainframe utilities. Engaging with competing vendors can provide viable replacement options, often with better cost options and support structures.

This transition will require upfront investment and careful change management. Users familiar with existing tools may resist change, but with good organizational change management, this can be overcome. It is a challenge, but it always pays off to replace overpriced tools and an unfavorable vendor relationship.

Now that you understand how MSU-based billing works, I will look at why this model poses challenges for organizations making business and technology decisions. These aren't theoretical problems. I've observed each of these scenarios in real implementations across different industries and organization sizes.

Challenges with traditional license models

Another special topic to discuss in the context of licensing is the challenges with the MLC model.

One usage number for everything makes everything expensive

A fundamental pricing challenge in z/OS environments is that most software products are charged based on the same peak 4-Hour Rolling Average (4HRA) MSU measurement. As previously discussed regarding mainframe software costs, this 4HRA calculation encompasses the entire LPAR's resource usage.

This creates an inequitable pricing scenario: if product A's intensive usage drives the LPAR peak to 100 MSUs, and product B sees minimal utilization within the same LPAR, both products incur charges based on the 100 MSU peak. The billing mechanism doesn't differentiate between heavily utilized and rarely used software—all are subject to the same peak measurement. This results in disproportionate costs for lightly used components, as their pricing doesn't reflect their actual resource consumption.

Some specialized software tools operate as exceptions with individual measurement capabilities, where billing is based on that specific product's 4HRA usage value rather than the entire LPAR. However, this more equitable pricing approach remains unavailable for the majority of mainframe software products.

Usage increase may have unexpected results

Another challenge with monthly license charge (MLC) pricing is that increased z/OS workloads directly impact software costs. While this aligns with pay-per-use principles—where business growth naturally leads to higher resource utilization and corresponding vendor charges—the mainframe implementation differs significantly from modern cloud models.

The critical distinction lies in the shared nature of the mainframe environment. When one application experiences substantial growth and increases system resource consumption, it triggers cost increases across all software components, not just those related to the growing application. This architecture means that significant expansion in a single application can disproportionately inflate the entire platform's licensing costs, potentially making business growth financially prohibitive. The shared platform establishes a shared cost structure, where all applications share the financial burden of any individual application's increased usage.

Therefore, when you expect such significant increases, you should talk to your software vendors to prevent surprises.

An inhibitor for innovation

Another challenge with MLC licensing is that implementing business and technology innovations on the mainframe can lead to unexpected cost increases. The MLC pricing structure was established during periods of relatively stable usage patterns, creating a baseline that is now ill-suited for today's dynamic workloads. Modern initiatives typically demand significantly more computing resources than traditional workloads, making these innovations financially prohibitive when combined with the already high baseline pricing.

Consider the case of an insurance company that transformed its operations to a self-service model through a customer-facing web application. This implementation substantially increased the number of policy information retrieval and update transactions on their z/OS-based policy administration system. The resulting spike in monthly peak 4HRA measurements was so dramatic that it negated the business case for the entire initiative.

Again, consultation with your vendor is crucial when planning any expansion of mainframe usage. Many providers now offer alternative licensing models specifically designed for new workloads, often at more competitive rates than traditional MLC structures. For additional information on these options, refer to the section on *New License Models: Opportunities and* Pitfalls.

Mainframe hardware and software cost summary

MAINFRAME COST AT A GLANCE	
Software:	~66% of total cost
Hardware:	~17% of total cost
Management:	~17% of total cost
Key insight: Understanding MSU and 4HRA is critical to controlling your largest expense.	

Software costs dominate your mainframe costs. Understanding how this billing works is essential to controlling your largest cost component.

The following table summarizes the cost components identified in the previous sections.

Cost item		Account type
Capacity entitlement		Asset (intangible)
Server hardware	CPU	Asset
	Memory	Asset
	Other components	Asset
	Maintenance	Expense
Storage hardware	Disk	Asset
	Tape	Asset
	Maintenance	Expense
Connectivity	Network and SAN equipment	Asset
	Maintenance	Expense
Software	MLC software	Expense
	OTC software	Asset
	OTC Subscription and support	Expense

Chapter 16 Mainframes in the Cloud Era

Many organizations have adopted cloud strategies to offload IT infrastructure management to third-party providers, boosting agility, options, and ideally reducing costs.

Why can't we do this on the mainframe? We can, but. Mainframe platforms and applications, evolved over decades, rarely follow modern industry standards and often lack updates or standardized processes.

The transition to cloud-like IT requires new automation and standardization, plus targeted efforts to transform legacy systems—including z/OS and other apps—to align with cloud goals.

This chapter explores reaping benefits from both worlds via strategic integration, examined from three angles:

- Bringing cloud ease-of-use to the mainframe via "mainframe like a hyperscaler" (I am borrowing this term from an IT executive's strategy).
- Transforming infrastructure and applications for hyperscaler-like mainframe benefits.
- Building hybrid architectures with on-prem and cloud platforms.

Mainframe like a hyperscaler

The big benefit of doing IT in the cloud is its ease-of-use. It is easy to develop and change applications in the cloud.

Relatively easy, I should not exaggerate. In the cloud, we also have nitty-gritty details like VPCs with CIDR blocks and subnets, overlapping address ranges that suddenly break peering, security groups and NACLs with one wrong rule, Internet Gateways and NAT Gateways, and IAM policies that must line up before a single packet is allowed through.

But in the cloud, all services are standardized, and configurations can be automated. You can pick a service from a menu, and what it comprises is clearly defined and contained. These services can be configured through programming interfaces that you can use to build your infrastructure as code.

Such radical standardization and simplification are a prerequisite for achieving a cloud-like mainframe platform. Mainframe-like-a-hyperscaler requires standardized, simplified services that can be configured as code.

The problem with z/OS application environments: no (industry) standardization

For platforms like Linux and Windows, standardization is largely complete. However, this is not the case with z/OS application platforms.

An example. In Windows, you cannot change the names of C:\Windows or C:\Program Files. Similarly, you cannot alter /usr/bin or /bin on Linux. In z/OS, though, you can change the equivalents. You can have a SYS1.LINKLIB—a library similar to /bin in Linux, but you can also change its name to ACME.LINKLIB. In z/OS, you can modify almost everything.

Anything that can be changed will be changed. And it has. Most organizations utilizing z/OS sites have heavily customized their configurations. z/OS sites maintain their own naming standards for nearly every component: datasets, users, disks, parameter files, scripts, and script libraries.

Mainframe like a hyperscaler: a new approach to mainframe operations

To achieve this hyperscaler vision, we must be willing to change how mainframe environments are managed and governed. This means embracing standardization, radical simplification, treating everything as code, and adopting a DevOps mindset in which infrastructure, configuration, and operational procedures are all automated, versioned, and continuously improved as part of the delivery lifecycle.

Towards an industry standard

To transition z/OS toward a cloud model, organizations must establish clear standards and migrate infrastructure and applications to meet them. Leading mainframe vendors, including IBM, Broadcom, Rocket Software, BMC, HCL, and others, should lead by creating a unified z/OS platform standard and encouraging customer collaboration through an "open-source-like" model that all can adopt.

Standards would drive simplification by eliminating unnecessary customization options that currently overload z/OS. Many of these can be safely dropped to streamline operations and align with cloud agility goals.

Adopting a local standard

You cannot simply wait for industry-wide standards. Adopt your own rigorous standards now. Mainframes often started with standardized setups, but decades of evolution created unmaintained drift. This technical debt blocks progress.

Standardizing your environment is the essential starting point. Automation works only on standardized setups, and combining standardization, legacy removal, and automation enables cloud-like agility. I will discuss other aspects of technical debt and how to address this in Chapter Transformation strategies

Automation of infrastructure management: infrastructure as code

Like the application CICD processes, all infrastructure provisioning and configuration must be automated to enable flexible, on-demand creation and modification of infrastructure for your applications.

When infrastructure setups are standardized and automation is implemented, the code that automates infrastructure processes must be created in a similar manner to applications-as-code. There is no room anymore to do things manually. Everything should be codified.

In practice, we see that this is not always possible yet due to technical limitations. We depend on infrastructure suppliers for hardware, operating systems, and middleware. Not all hardware and middleware software are equipped with sufficient automation capabilities. Instead, these tools depend on human processes. Suppliers should shift their focus from developing sleek user interfaces to providing modern, likely declarative, interfaces that enable the use of tools in an infra-as-code process.

DevOps principles

For applications, CI/CD pipelines serve as the codebases for application creation. Similarly, *infrastructure pipelines* serve as the foundation for reliable infrastructure code. Definitions of the infrastructure making up the environment must be treated like code and managed in a source code management system, where they can be properly versioned. The code must be tested in a test environment before being deployed to production.

A culture change

In many organizations, infrastructure management teams are among the last to adopt agile working methods. They have always been so focused on keeping the show on the road that the risks of continuity disruptions have prevented management from having teams focus on development infrastructure-as-code.

Also, the infrastructure staff are often relatively conservative about automating their manual tasks. Usually, that is not because they do not want it, but because they are so concerned about disruptions that they would rather get up at 3 a.m. to make a manual change than risk a programming mistake in the automation infra-as-code solution.

When moving towards infrastructure-as-code, the concerns of the infrastructure department management and staff should be taken seriously. Their continuity concerns can often be used to create extra robust infrastructure as a code solution. What I have seen, for example, is that staff do not just worry about creating infra-as-code changes but are most concerned about scenarios in which something could go wrong. Their ideas for rolling back changes have often been eye-opening, offering a reliable solution that not only automates happy scenarios but also addresses unhappy ones.

However, concern for robustness is not an excuse to keep processes as they are. Infrastructure management teams should also recognize that there is less risk in relying on good automation than in having individuals execute complex configuration tasks manually.

The evolving tooling landscape

The mainframe ecosystem now offers a growing set of tools to support infrastructure provisioning, with solutions like z/OSMF, Ansible, Terraform, and Zowe rapidly evolving. However, despite this progress, the landscape remains fragmented, lacking a unified, vision-driven architecture to guide its integration.

Efforts are underway, led by IBM and other software vendors, to enhance these tools and bridge the gap with cross-platform provisioning frameworks such as Kubernetes and OpenShift. Notably, Ansible for z/OS is gaining traction as a key enabler for automation.

Figure 60 provides an overview of the technical architecture of an infrastructure automation tooling. It clarifies which tools are best suited for specific provisioning tasks. While significant work remains, there are significant advancements in the tooling landscape and we must adopt these new technologies.

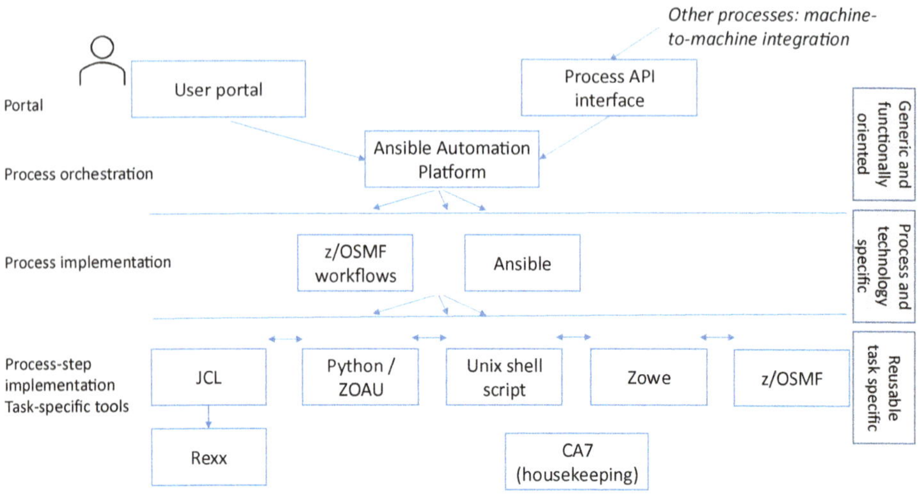

Figure 60 An example of an automation tooling framework for z/OS

The approach to a cloud-like mainframe

Mainframe legacy infrastructure and applications must be transformed into standardized services to enable the use of cloud-like features. The discussion above focused on the infrastructure-as-code approach; there is more to consider to reap all the benefits of a cloud-like approach.

A stepwise approach to standardization

A standardization program should encompass the following aspects. These points are not specific to the mainframe. I have seen cloud application deployments suffer from the adoption of automation and governance. Without these management and cost of your cloud application can easily spiral out of control. Having cloud-like foundation capabilities is not enough.

- Standardize the application platform.

Define an application standard, then ensure all your applications adhere to the same architecture and standards. This might be the most critical effort in your transformation journey if your application portfolio is significantly neglected.

- Automate application deployments.

Create automated procedures for deploying applications and changes to the standardized application platform. However, standardize first; otherwise, your automation may become tangled in a web of code accommodating deviations and exceptions.

- Automate test data provisioning.

Recognize that good data provisioning is a prerequisite for good testing. Tests are useless if the data on which these tests are based do not reflect real-life situations.

- Automate testing.

Testing can be part of a CI/CD pipeline, but more thorough testing is often done continuously. Once you can continuously deploy application changes and ensure test data is high-quality, you can implement continuous testing. Application deployments and test data refreshes can run daily, with testing running overnight.

- Automate middleware provisioning.

Automate your middleware provisioning. This will improve speed and quality and address the need for speed to fix vulnerabilities in middleware components, as the 2021 log4j issues illustrated.

- Automated operating system provisioning.

Automate operating system provisioning using the same logic as for your middleware.

- Automate everything, all operations and management.

All processes should be automated, and zero-touch and self-service should become standard. A service can be executed manually twice, but it should be automated by the third time.

Congratulations. You should now be able to deploy your mainframe application everywhere: on-prem, in the cloud, or in the data center of the company you just acquired.

Hybrid Cloud Architecture Patterns

In the previous sections, I have discussed how we can transform the mainframe to function like a cloud, with its benefits of easy service consumption.

Still, there is no black-and-white choice between running your application on the mainframe or in the cloud. Organizations do not have to choose between the options; they integrate both. The question isn't "mainframe or cloud?", or “on-prem or cloud” in more generic terms, but rather "which workloads belong where, and how do we connect them effectively?"

Based on implementations across the financial services, insurance, and government sectors, I summarize three common architectural patterns that I have found to be both practical and proven.

Pattern 1: Cloud-first for front-end and Mainframe for core applications

This is a common pattern for organizations with business-critical applications deployed on the mainframe. Customer-facing applications and rapidly changing business logic run in the cloud, while high-volume transaction processing and systems of record remain on the mainframe.

Pattern overview

The cloud layer handles three primary functions:

- User engagement applications such as Web portals, mobile applications, and customer service interfaces deployed in AWS, Azure, or Google Cloud

- Experience layer applications such as APIs, user authentication, session management, and personalization engines
- Agile business logic, like quickly evolving business rules, product catalogs, and content management systems

The mainframe layer handles:

- Transaction processing such as account updates, policy changes, payment processing, anything requiring high volume, low latency, secure transactions with and high integrity guarantees.
- Core data management for critical data like customer accounts, policy records, transaction history, and your systems of record.
- Batch processing applications like end-of-day processing, regulatory reporting, and data consolidation.

There may be a mid-tier of applications sitting between the engagement applications and the backend applications. These mid-office applications can be in the cloud, or on-premise on distributed or mainframe platforms, depending on non-functional, regulatory, resilience, and other requirements we will see in section 'The Balancing Act' in the next chapter.

Integration approach

Integration occurs through REST APIs exposed by mainframe applications (using tools such as z/OS Connect) and consumed by cloud-native applications. The cloud applications never directly access mainframe databases. All interactions flow through well-defined service interfaces.

Message queuing may provide asynchronous communication for non-time-critical updates, allowing systems to operate independently and handle temporary network disruptions.

Application

This pattern works best when you have stable, high-volume core processes, combined with more quickly evolving customer experiences.

A European insurance company successfully implemented this pattern: their 30-year-old policy administration system remained on the mainframe while they built a modern, cloud-based customer portal that handles 2 million interactions daily. The integration layer processes 50,000 API calls per hour with 99.95% availability.

Pattern 2: Data Lake federation

Some organizations need to combine mainframe data with data from distributed and cloud applications for analytics or reporting workloads. Rather than replicating all mainframe data to the cloud, which is an expensive and complex approach, you can implement a federated data architecture.

Pattern overview

A data virtualization layer (see also section Access via a data virtualization layer) sits between analytics tools and various data sources. This layer provides a unified view without physically moving data until it is needed for analysis.

For mainframe integration:

- Real-time queries: Selected data is accessed via JDBC/ODBC connections to Db2 for z/OS databases. To this end, (virtual) historical databases are instantiated. This ensures that these queries do not interfere with business-critical transactional workloads.
- Periodic extracts: Batch processes extract changed data to cloud-based data lakes.
- Event streaming: Critical data changes flow through Kafka to keep replicas in the cloud up to date.

The analytics platform can be in the cloud (for example, Databricks, Snowflake, or a cloud data warehouse). It queries this federated layer, and the virtualization software determines whether to fetch data from the mainframe or use cloud-based replicas.

Application

This pattern is applied when you need to analyze mainframe data alongside data from other sources without disrupting operational systems. A retail bank uses this approach to combine 40 years of transaction history from its mainframe with recent digital banking data for customer analytics. Their data science teams access everything through a single interface without having to know where data physically resides.

Pattern 3: Hybrid processing with workload placement

You can also apply a decision pattern with dynamic placement decisions. With this, each application component runs where it performs best and costs least, with the flexibility to move workloads as needs change.

Pattern overview

Applications are designed as collections of loosely coupled components or microservices. Placement rules determine where each component runs:

- Mainframe for high-volume transactional components, components requiring extreme reliability, and services tightly coupled to mainframe systems of record data.
- Cloud for specific compute-intensive analytics, variable-demand workloads, and components requiring rapid scaling,
- Portable: Services designed to run on either platform, moved based on cost and performance metrics.

Container orchestration with OpenShift across IBM Z, other on-premises platforms, and cloud platforms can provide a consistent deployment model. Services communicate through APIs and message queues, making physical location transparent.

Application

This pattern is most suitable for organizations with mature DevOps practices and applications designed (or redesigned) for portability. A telecommunications company rebuilt its billing system this way: core rating engines run on the mainframe (processing 500 million events daily), while usage analytics and customer notifications run in the cloud. During month-end processing, additional workloads temporarily shift to the mainframe to leverage its parallel processing capabilities.

Choosing a pattern

Your choice depends on different aspects. If you want to integrate existing applications, Pattern 1 is a good choice. Patterns 2 and 3 require more architectural maturity.

If your business drivers are a driving factor, then the customer experience focus would fit with Pattern 1. If your focus is on analytics, Pattern 2 is a good choice. Cost optimization and flexibility are best addressed in Pattern 3.

Technical capabilities may also drive your choice. Pattern 1 requires solid API design. Pattern 2 needs data architecture expertise. Pattern 3 is best with advanced DevOps and cloud-native skills.

Most organizations start with Pattern 1, evolve to Pattern 2 for analytics needs, and gradually adopt Pattern 3 elements as applications are modernized. There's no requirement to choose just one. Different application portfolios can use different patterns based on their specific needs.

A Financial Model for Cloud and Mainframe

A critical hurdle to realizing the benefits of the cloud is the licensing model imposed by software suppliers. Most existing financial models for mainframe software hinder cloud adoption. For example, current models lack flexibility and, at best, offer a pay-per-use option based on the four-hour rolling average (4HRA) (see the section The cost of mainframe software). This makes continuous development and testing prohibitively expensive under traditional pricing structures.

In short, a new pricing model must be developed and agreed upon to enable true cloud-like adoption in mainframe environments.

Conclusion

Many organizations are automating IT processes, many of which stem from rigorous automation initiatives. The push towards cloud-like computing necessitates standardizing and automating IT processes.

We need to adopt the automation agenda to meet the speed and quality requirements we need today. For mainframes, this means prioritizing standardization across z/OS platforms, middleware, and applications to enable cloud-like self-service and portability. Without industry-wide standards and a simplified platform, automation remains cumbersome in certain areas.

I have presented hybrid architecture patterns for a pragmatic path forward. You keep core transactional workloads where they are best catered for: on mainframes for reliability and cost efficiency at scale. You deploy applications in the cloud for agile front-ends, analytics via data virtualization, and specific variable workloads. A cost framework allows your organization to guide placement decisions objectively. Cloud-era mainframes thrive by integration. With this approach, you standardize now to deploy anywhere tomorrow.

Chapter 17 Transformation strategies

In Chapter Modern mainframe application architectures, I sketched an ideal world, described a modern z/OS application, discussed how to design decoupled applications effectively, and how to build hybrid architectures.

Unfortunately, on a platform as old as z/OS, we find applications that are not designed with modern-day insights. An application's architecture has probably been modified over the years, and an even less-ideal architecture has evolved. A backlog of technical debt has accumulated, and keeping the application in sync with business needs is becoming increasingly complex.

In this chapter, I will look at the various forms of technical debt your mainframe environment may suffer from and what you can do about them. I will discuss how you can assess the technological changes and the efforts needed to get your mainframe applications ready for the future. Next, I will look at the options you have to either replace the mainframe platform or invest in bringing it up to a state fit for your organization's future.

A problem for the organization

Many organizations struggle with isolated, expensive, and complex mainframe environments that consume a significant portion of their IT budgets. Consequently, decisions about mainframe investments are often made at the board level. However, assessing whether the value of these investments aligns with the business value the platform delivers is usually very complex. Mainframe applications are typically core systems deeply embedded in organizational processes, making replacement both expensive and complicated.

At the same time, organizations find that legacy applications and outdated technology severely limit their capacity for business innovation. Too much effort is spent on maintenance and continuity, leaving little room for innovation. Organizational and technical debt continues to build up in the mainframe environment, modernization is postponed, and the workforce is aging. Meanwhile, new technologies are being deployed to accelerate IT support for business innovation, and organizations are moving toward cloud-based IT. Agile methods for software delivery are being adopted, but the mismatch between Enterprise Architecture and the mainframe landscape is growing each year. Senior management and enterprise architects are left wondering how to position the mainframe in this evolving context.

A decision must be made: whether to replace the mainframe legacy or revitalize the environment. However, decision makers often lack the complete information needed to make a sound judgment.

Technical debt

Old mainframe application platforms often carry technical debt across multiple areas. First, the applications themselves may have been poorly maintained over the years. Secondly, parts of the mainframe infrastructure, operating system, and middleware software may be outdated. I will discuss the different forms of technical debt and how to address them.

Application technical debt

Mainframe applications may face specific legacy issues. These make applications difficult to maintain and are operational risks when making changes, such as upgrading z/OS and middleware. I will discuss typical problems found in a mainframe application landscape.

Assembler language

One of the first issues in problematic mainframe applications is the use of Assembler language programs, which often rely on deprecated operating system routines. More than 25 years ago, writing custom Assembler programs was a common practice to achieve technical tasks that were impossible with the programming languages available at the time.

Today, however, these limitations no longer exist. All the functionality once requiring Assembler programs can now be achieved using modern, supported alternatives. The continued use of Assembler language poses significant risks: expertise in assembler is scarce, and these routines frequently depend on sensitive or outdated programming interfaces that may already be deprecated or at risk of becoming so.

For every historical limitation, future-proof alternatives are now available. Phasing out Assembler language should be a priority to reduce risk, improve maintainability, and ensure long-term sustainability.

Old executables

Old mainframe applications often consist of programs that have not been compiled for decades. z/OS provides fantastic *backward compatibility*. The drawback of this backward compatibility is that program code that has not been touched for a long time still works. The compiled code with machine instructions for 40-year-old machinery still runs on modern 64-bit mainframes, making mainframe application owners complacent.

The problem is that these executables use the mainframe instruction set from 30 years ago and are inefficient. More importantly, the risk with these programs is that they cannot be compiled with modern compilers. So, you may find yourself in a challenging situation when changes are needed.

Another issue with these old programs is that the executable's source code may be lost, or, if it exists, it is difficult to determine whether it is the correct version.

All in all, maintaining these old executables will require extensive testing.

Dependency on outdated programming languages and middleware

It is not only assembler skills that are becoming very scarce. You still find old, niche programming environments and accompanying runtime tools in mainframe environments. I do not mean COBOL or PL/I here, but niche 4GL tools and frameworks, such as CA Gen, EGL, Focus, AppBuilder, and Cool:Gen. You may also find outdated middleware tools still in use in applications. Some software vendors have even given customers the source code of their old compilers they no longer wish to support, enabling their clients to maintain the middleware themselves and keep their legacy applications running.

You must either decommission or properly maintain any legacy application programming language, as it poses a continuity risk for your applications in the short- or medium-term.

Home-grown frameworks and middleware

Another common issue in problematic applications stems from a development practice found in many organizations: building custom technical frameworks, middleware tools, or extending the operating system with proprietary functionality. This is not just a challenge unique to mainframes but a broader issue across all platforms, including Java, Python, and other modern languages. Applications in these languages often include layers of utility packages that, over time, can create significant maintainability challenges. The mainframe, with its long history, is particularly susceptible to this problem.

These homegrown tools and frameworks are often hard to maintain. Many were originally written in assembler language and rely on outdated technologies or unsupported interfaces, which only exacerbates the maintenance burden. Over time, these custom solutions become technical debt, complicating updates, increasing risk, and consuming valuable resources.

Infrastructure technical debt

Infrastructure components in z/OS environments may suffer from legacy issues, such as the application problems we have seen above.

Outdated and unsupported tools

We find that unsupported tools are still in use on the infrastructure side. While maintenance of the tools is delayed, the tools are never retired.

Here, we also see that the software supplier prefers to hand over the source code rather than continue maintaining the product. Of course, this only masks the operational risk these tools pose to the organization and is, at best, a short-term solution.

Home-grown middleware and tools

Similar to what was practiced in application development, in the past, it was not uncommon to build custom middleware solutions and system administration tools. The knowledge of these custom-built tools disappeared with the retirement of the staff that created the middleware, leaving the organization with a huge problem.

Customizations of the operating system and middleware

IBM and other software vendors on the mainframe have historically provided many options to augment or modify the z/OS operating system and middleware tools with custom code. Many so-called exit points were created where an organization could insert its functionality, mostly in assembler language.

These modifications are written in assembler language and, therefore, increasingly difficult to maintain. Because the need for these modifications has disappeared, you should remove them.

Case Study: Addressing Mainframe Skills Risk Through Assembler Modernization

A large organization with a long-standing reliance on mainframe systems faced a growing concern: the specialized knowledge required to maintain and modify Assembler code and system customizations was concentrated among a small group of senior system programmers. With these experts approaching retirement, the organization recognized a significant risk to the continuity and stability of its critical operations.

To mitigate this risk, the organization initiated a structured program to reduce its dependence on Assembler. The first step involved a comprehensive analysis of their Assembler portfolio. This review helped identify which programs were still in use, their specific functions, and whether they could be replaced or rewritten in COBOL.

The results were clear: all Assembler-based application programs could be decommissioned if no longer necessary, or rewritten in COBOL without losing any functionality. This transition eliminated the need for Assembler expertise in day-to-day operations, making the system more accessible to a broader range of developers.

For system-level customizations in Assembler, the process was more complex due to the integration of these components with core system functions. However, the organization removed 80% of these dependencies, thereby simplifying the remaining codebase. The remaining 20% consisted of straightforward, non-critical functions that were either scheduled for future replacement or thoroughly documented to ensure knowledge transfer.

This modernization effort not only reduced operational risk but also improved the long-term maintainability of the mainframe environment. By adopting a proactive approach that combined detailed analysis with incremental replacement, the organization successfully addressed a critical skills gap while future-proofing its systems.

Technical debt is the neglect of maintenance

Much of the technical debt in mainframe environments stems, let me be blunt, from maintenance neglect. Application and infrastructure specialists frequently alert management to the need to refactor applications and update infrastructure. However, these critical activities are often postponed in favor of addressing more immediate business priorities.

In agile methodologies, it is widely recognized that accumulating technical debt slows development velocity. Addressing this debt is theoretically an integral part of agile workflows, but in practice, it can be challenging to prioritize. For z/OS environments burdened with significant technical debt, extra effort is often required to restore the platform to a healthy state. Deciding whether the investment is worthwhile or if the debt has grown too large requires careful evaluation. The technical gap must be assessed in relation to the application's business value and the cost of maintaining the platform. Only then can a well-informed decision be made.

Another important consideration is that renovating existing applications on the z/OS platform is a viable, often-overlooked modernization strategy. Organizations that assume new applications must be built exclusively on cloud platforms using the latest tools have a limited view of modernization. Cloud platforms, while innovative, are still relatively unproven and may require significant rework over time as technologies evolve. For example, even a 10-year-old Java application requires substantial maintenance to keep pace with Java's ongoing updates. The key takeaway is this: *inaction is not an option*. Leaving old applications unattended only deepens technical debt and risk.

In the following sections, I will explore key considerations for sunsetting the mainframe platform and outline an approach to rejuvenating the mainframe application platform.

What to do if you want to decommission the mainframe

Deciding to leave the mainframe platform is not easy. Regardless of how you approach it, a significant investment in transformation is necessary.

There are several approaches to decommissioning. I will discuss the main approaches here and add some remarks. A comprehensive solution will likely combine these options, depending on application characteristics and business needs.

Outsourcing infrastructure management

Outsourcing means you hand over the management of your mainframe infrastructure to a specialized supplier.

From a technical perspective, nothing changes. This option removes the mainframe assets from your balance sheets and relieves you of responsibility for infrastructure management.

The company taking over your infrastructure management may or may not be enthusiastic about modernizing your legacy. Additionally, you will still need development and application support personnel for your mainframe applications unless you also outsource that function. When your applications suffer from technical debt and inflexibility, this option will not resolve this. Outsourcing is a financial and staffing solution. Nothing changes technically. In return, you get supplier management, which is also not to be underestimated.

Rehost the platform

With a rehosting approach, you remove your mainframe applications from the IBM hardware and operating system and migrate them to another platform.

Figure 61 Rehosting legacy

Rehosting is a technically complex operation. Several service providers offer solutions to support this approach. Most rehosting solutions emulate your mainframe middleware stack on a commodity application server and database management system hosted on a Windows or Linux server. Your mainframe applications can then be migrated to this emulated mainframe platform. The idea is that your applications and data remain largely untouched. Only the underlying hardware and software stack is replaced.

Migration activities can be very significant. Although the idea is that your applications remain untouched, modifications are always necessary. Even when minimal changes are needed, application testing and data migration require a significant amount of time and effort.

Rehosting lets you eliminate the mainframe infrastructure. However, you will still need the mainframe application skills to develop and maintain your mainframe applications. You will also still need specific skills to run and maintain the newly introduced emulation layer and platform.

As with the outsourcing option, if your mainframe applications suffer from technical debt and become too inflexible for your organization, this option does not help you address this issue. The effect may well be the opposite, as more complexity is added to the configuration.

In any case, the rehosting option is only a temporary solution. If you decide on this path, the next step is still to retire or replace the application's functionality.

Retire all applications on the mainframe platform

The cleanest solution may seem to be retiring all mainframe applications. However, this option is only viable if alternative applications are readily available and a timely, complete migration is feasible. Many organizations have attempted this path, only to find themselves stuck halfway through the migration process. The result is the worst of both worlds: maintaining two applications for the same functionality, doubling costs, complexity, and operational risk.

Replace through repurchase

Another option is to replace custom mainframe applications with off-the-shelf solutions, whether deployed on-premises or as SaaS (Software-as-a-Service). However, this approach is only viable if the package's standard functionality aligns with your business requirements. In larger organizations, this is rarely the case. Often, significant time and resources are spent customizing these packages to meet specific organizational needs, introducing new complexities.

Additionally, migration to the new application must be carefully planned to avoid creating an even more fragmented and complex IT landscape than the one you started with. Without proper planning, the result can be increased costs, operational inefficiencies, and technical debt.

Replace through refactoring

Another replacement option is to refactor your existing applications. Refactoring is particularly valuable when your applications include custom features that are not available in off-the-shelf solutions. This approach involves rebuilding legacy application functionality into modern components on new middleware, hardware, or cloud-based platforms.

While refactoring requires significant development and migration efforts, it offers greater control over the migration process and enables a more realistic, achievable timeline.

Figure 62 Refactoring legacy applications

Do nothing

The one option you cannot afford to choose is inaction.

Regardless of your long-term strategy, it is critical to avoid accumulating more technical debt in your mainframe environment. This means keeping hardware and software versions up to date and actively executing a plan to address existing technical debt.

Too many organizations neglect maintenance of their legacy mainframe environments, only to face exorbitant costs when forced to catch up or retire systems under pressure. In some cases, this neglect leads to real business disruptions, as outdated IT systems stifle innovation and agility. I have even seen organizations forced to shut down parts of their business because of prolonged inaction.

The message is clear: doing nothing is not an option. Proactive maintenance and modernization are essential to avoid costly consequences and ensure your IT infrastructure supports rather than hinders your business goals.

Investing in modernization

As demonstrated in the previous chapter, modernizing the mainframe into an agile platform is not only possible but practical, thanks to its modern features and tools. Many organizations prefer this approach over retirement, as it provides greater flexibility to take the right steps at the right time.

However, the cost of modernization depends heavily on the current state of your mainframe environment. Organizations that have neglected maintenance for a decade or more often face a massive backlog of technical debt. In some cases, the backlog becomes so overwhelming that divestment is the only viable option.

Case Study: Middleware neglect forces costly core rebuild

An organization needed to support business applications in multiple languages, including Chinese and Russian. After years of neglecting middleware maintenance, they were unable to upgrade to versions that support Unicode or DBCS for Chinese and Russian. As a result, they were forced to rebuild their core applications from scratch, delaying business innovation and incurring substantial costs.

This case highlights the hidden risks of deferred maintenance in mainframe ecosystems, where incompatible character encoding blocked business expansion into multilingual markets.

Modernization is not a one-time project but a stepwise improvement process. It requires holistic changes across multiple areas, including:

- Adjusting the application portfolio to align with business needs,
- Updating architecture to support agility and scalability,
- Refreshing application and infrastructure technology to meet current standards,
- Modernizing DevOps processes and tools to accelerate delivery.

This may sound like standard application lifecycle management. It is. Your mainframe applications must be managed with the same rigor and attention as the rest of your application portfolio. Neglecting them is no longer an option in today's fast-paced digital landscape.

Can't we move to the Cloud?

I have not discussed the option to move your z/OS applications "as-is" to the cloud. This is because such an option does not exist for z/OS applications. A z/OS platform in the cloud is simply not available.

A few suppliers offer mainframe Infrastructure as a Service, but these solutions are limited and primarily intended for software vendors that require a z/OS development platform. IBM provides a Platform as a Service for development environments that appears to be hosted primarily on an emulation product: the IBM Z Development and Test Environment (ZD&T). However, this solution is challenging to manage, does not scale effectively, and is therefore unsuitable for serious production deployments.

A Program to regain control of your Mainframe platform

To determine the best strategy for your organization, whether divesting or modernizing, several key aspects should be considered. These aspects aim to bring the mainframe platform back into strategic IT focus and enable informed decisions about the platform and the applications it hosts.

Get clarity on the cost and value of the Mainframe and its applications

The cost of the mainframe platform is usually straightforward to establish. As a centralized platform, it is relatively easy to calculate its operational hardware and software costs, especially compared to distributed platforms, where costs are often spread across many components and organizational units. However, gaining insight into the total software and management costs on distributed platforms is not easy.

While the total cost of the mainframe platform is relatively easy to understand, calculating the cost of individual applications running on the mainframe is more challenging. Even more difficult is gaining insight into the value of these applications compared to the costs of alternatives on other platforms, including cloud solutions.

Understanding these cost and benefit figures is necessary to make informed investment or divestment decisions. Often, applications are marked as "legacy" and targeted for replacement without evaluating their true business value or the actual cost of replacement. Such implicit choices can be costly and painful. You must prevent them.

Position the Mainframe Platform in Your IT Landscape

Mainframe applications must have a clear role in your IT landscape. In many organizations, the mainframe is seen as the old machine in the corner of the data center that runs some backend applications essential for the business, but no one can clearly articulate its strategic role.

Defining the mainframe's position within an organization guides IT planning, supports enterprise architecture development, and informs strategic application integration scenarios and application development roadmaps. In most organizations running a mainframe, the platform is positioned as the robust solution for systems of record, serving high-volume, standardized backend services.

The Balancing Act

Positioning your computing platforms nowadays requires weighing many factors; technique and cost are not the only ones. We have seen in Chapter 15 Understanding mainframe cost, that you considered the *real* cost: operational expenses, modernization investments, and the long-term value it delivers.

Other factors to consider include:

- Staffing. Can you hire the people you need to run the IT to support your business?
- Portability. This is true for both on-prem and cloud platforms. Your existing on-prem or cloud platform might not be the best choice for next year. With technologies such as Kubernetes and OpenShift, workloads can move between cloud and on-premises environments. This gives you the flexibility required in today's fast-changing world and regulatory landscape.
- Non-functional requirements: availability, scalability, integrity, robustness, and security. Seamless scaling isn't optional. Data

integrity and consistency are not eventual. These are the foundations of trust and compliance.

- Geopolitics and related compliance requirements. Data sovereignty and regulatory compliance are increasingly important, especially in highly regulated industries and government sectors.
- Cyber resilience. It's not enough to defend against threats; you need to anticipate, respond, and recover.

Many of these aspects have been discussed in this book. I have not discussed staffing, but I will address it in section Building your mainframe talent pipeline.

Comparison: when Cloud, when Mainframe

The mainframe-versus-cloud debate often generates more heat than resolutions. The reality is more nuanced than the discussions. Neither platform is universally cheaper or better. The optimal choice depends on workload characteristics, volumes, and operational requirements.

I have created a framework for making informed and objective decisions. I also realize that such a framework may lead to debate. Use it as such, or change it to your preference, as long as you evaluate objectively along the different factors.

The Cost Comparison Framework

When evaluating platforms for a specific workload, consider these five dimensions:

Factor	When Mainframe	When Cloud	Rationale
Transaction Volume and latency	>1M transactions/day with predictable patterns	Variable or unpredictable volumes, <500K transactions/day	Mainframe pricing rewards steady, high-volume workloads. Cloud pricing suits variable demand.
Data Characteristics	Large, structured datasets requiring ACID properties	Unstructured data, streaming data, or data lakes	Mainframe databases excel at transactional integrity. Cloud platforms handle diverse data types better.
Change Frequency	Stable business logic, less frequent changes	Rapid iteration, continuous deployment	Cloud enables faster iteration cycles at lower risk.
Latency and availability	Low-latency transactional workloads. Tightly coupled to systems of record	Loosely coupled, API-driven architecture	Co-location reduces latency and integration complexity and significantly improves availability across a critical chain.
Compliance Requirements	Stringent audit trails, data residency requirements, top-class cyber resilience	Standard cloud compliance is sufficient	Mainframe security and compliance features are integrated, mature, and comprehensive. Stringent data residency and resilience requirements drive mainframe placement.

Analyze the Mainframe application portfolio status and strategic fit

Many of your mainframe applications originated decades ago, so reassessing their lifecycle status and their technical, functional, and strategic fit in the organization is necessary. The mainframe applications may be nearing the end of their lifecycle and severely lack strategic functionality or technical capabilities.

The gap between strategic fit and the current state may be so significant that the only conclusion is that the platform does not fit the organization's goals.

Assess the technical vitality of your Mainframe platform

As discussed earlier, in some organizations, mainframe platforms and applications have long been neglected. This neglect may stem from the assumption that the platform will be phased out or simply from the fact that mainframe applications have remained under the radar of senior decision-makers.

Consequently, the technical state of the mainframe and the staff responsible for developing and maintaining the platform will need to be drastically rejuvenated.

Assess the operational effectiveness of DevOps and Infrastructure Teams

The state of the supporting organization may also drive decisions about the platform and its applications. In many organizations, the processes for developing and maintaining applications and infrastructure on the mainframe are based on outdated waterfall models that are ill-suited to a modern, agile organization.

DevOps processes must be modernized when the platform and its applications hold a strategic position within the organization. As described earlier, this is not so much a technical transformation but an organizational transformation.

Align the Mainframe platform with your cloud strategy

Almost all organizations today have a cloud strategy for at least part of their application portfolio. An assessment of the mainframe platform and the different needs for a cloud strategy may be needed. For example, new integration and security scenarios might be required for cloud-based engagement applications in concert with mainframe backend applications.

The Way Forward, with Senior Business Sponsorship

A thorough analysis of the topics covered in the previous sections should culminate in a comprehensive improvement plan for business alignment, architectural adjustments, and operational fit. Execution of this plan must be actively controlled by senior business and IT management.

A steering body is needed to address challenges quickly. Senior business and IT management, along with business and enterprise architects, must be part of the steering body to ensure that agreed-upon goals remain on target.

Building your mainframe talent pipeline

An important aspect of your transformation journey is your talent pipeline. Many organizations I have seen have neglected not only the maintenance of their technology but also their IT staff and the way they hire.

Case study: Rejuvenating the mainframe workforce

In 2022, a European organization posted a job opening for a "Mainframe Developer." They received three applications. The hiring manager was frustrated: "You cannot find any COBOL skills anymore."

The organization consulted a specialized recruiting firm, which reposted the same role under a different title: "Enterprise Application Engineer for high-volume business-critical transaction processing." The job was described as "building high-volume, super-reliable systems, exploring AI capabilities, processing millions of transactions per day, and using different programming platforms, including Python, Java, and yes, COBOL."

They received 47 applications in two weeks. All applicants were under 40.

Another organization realized that the average age of its mainframe staff was increasing by one year each year, and that it was already over 55. These people were running the organization's core business processes, and a quarter of them were going to retire within 5 years. This organization took a modern approach to rejuvenating its mainframe team, which I will describe in this section. Within 5 years, they reduced the average age by almost 10 years.

The mainframe doesn't have a talent problem. Your organization has a marketing problem.

Rewrite the narrative

When you are serious about staffing your mainframe teams, your job description should read: "We are building next-generation transaction-processing systems that handle 70% of the world's financial transactions. You will work with AI accelerators, containers, event streaming, and Python, alongside languages like COBOL, to process millions of operations per second. Your code will touch billions in currency every day. When it works, the national/global economy runs smoothly. When it breaks, it's front-page news." Adapt to your context, but replace "Mainframe Developer" with a description that excites modern engineers.

Rebrand the work

In job postings, focus on the modern stack: Docker/Kubernetes, Git, Jenkins, Ansible, Python, and Java, along with COBOL, AI/ML, GenAI, Kafka, REST APIs, VS Code, and modern IDEs.

Be clear and forward-looking: "You will work with technologies from multiple eras: proven COBOL systems processing millions of transactions alongside new Python-based AI models. Our platform runs everything from code written in 1985 to services deployed yesterday. That is not a bug; it is the reality of running systems that cannot fail."

Invest in modern tooling

If your developers are still primarily using ISPF and 3270 terminals in 2025, you are signaling "we do not invest in our people."

A minimum modern baseline is VS Code or Eclipse with z/OS extensions, Git for source control, automated CI/CD pipelines, GenAI-supported development and operations, and modern collaboration tools (Slack/Teams, Jira, Confluence).

Hire for potential, not experience

Look for strong problem-solving ability, programming fundamentals (in any language), curiosity and a learning mindset, communication skills, and a willingness to work with diverse technologies.

A smart developer can learn COBOL in weeks. She will not go to old-school week-long training classes but use tools like YouTube, Discord,

GitHub, and Stack Overflow. Hire smart people and teach them what they need to know.

Internal mobility programs

Your best source of mainframe talent might be sitting in your cloud team right now.

Cross-train existing developers: Java developers can learn mainframe Java (WebSphere Liberty), database experts can learn Db2 for z/OS, DevOps engineers can learn z/OS automation, and cloud architects can learn hybrid cloud architecture.

Benefits: existing employees understand the business, lower risk than external hiring, creates valuable cross-platform expertise, and costs less than external recruitment.

Partner with universities

Create internship programs. Fund scholarships. Provide training resources. Give guest lectures. This is modern-day hiring, not even specific to mainframes.

And IBM and other vendors offer academic programs. Use them. Build relationships with computer science departments. The students are interested. They often just do not know the opportunity exists.

Case study: From 3 to 27 students enrolled in the mainframe curriculum

A Belgian University of Applied Sciences offers a degree in Applied Computer Science and faced the same challenge many organizations face: making mainframe work appealing. A lecturer in the Computer Science department shares what changed:

"The bachelor's degree acts as a microcosm of the real-world job market, allowing students to choose from various specialisations during their studies. Specialisations like 'infrastructure engineer', ‘full stack developer’, and ‘AI and Data engineer’ are self-sustaining in terms of enrolments, as they align naturally with students' intrinsic interests. The mainframe curriculum requires a distinct approach, as ‘the mainframe’ is either unknown or carries a negative perception among the younger generation.”

Sound familiar? This is the same marketing problem we have been discussing. But instead of accepting it, the university took action.

The lecturer continues:

“Awareness, passion, and mindset are the cornerstones of success. Awareness helps students understand the impact of the mainframe on society, the technical sophistication behind it, and its critical role in keeping essential services running, planting the seeds of curiosity that can lead to a true passion.

The mindset is the only thing that cannot be taught or experienced. Students who successfully enter the mainframe job market tend to have a proven interest in back-end computing, a willingness to be mentored, and an eagerness to learn.”

By combining these key success factors with the broader mainframe educational ecosystem—hands-on training, work-based learning, mentoring, communities, hackathons, and events—the degree program became a distinctive and appealing option that effectively attracted and engaged students.

The results were spectacular. After years with only three students enrolled in the mainframe curriculum, they increased enrollment to 27, doubling the previous year's record. Paradoxically, they even had to turn students away.

Notice what worked: they did not wait for students to discover mainframes on their own. They actively created awareness, connected it to real impact, and built an ecosystem of support. The talent was always there. It just needed to be shown why this matters.

Empower the next generation

In 2019, Reg Harbeck wrote an excellent article in the magazine Destination Z, 'Overcoming IBM Z Inertia.' In this article, Harbeck encourages IBM Z (mainframe) users to modernize their mainframe.

Harbeck describes the path of action as recruiting new mainframers, assigning them to identify and document the expected capabilities of current mainframe solutions, and working with the organization to determine what needs to be retired, replaced, or contained.

In other words, Harbeck suggests tasking a new generation with the mainframe portfolio renewal and not leaving this to the old generation, who are "surviving until they retire while rocking the boat as little as possible" -hard words from Harbeck to get people in action.

In addition, *it is essential to ensure senior management support to prevent day-to-day priorities from watering down the priority of a rejuvenation program*. Also, with close management attention, you ensure that perceived or real roadblocks are addressed resolutely.

Furthermore, modernization efforts should be organized separately from day-to-day operations to minimize overlap with operational demands. Appoint a senior management and a senior technical executive with a strong mainframe affiliation to mentor, guide, and support the young team from an organizational and strategic perspective. Have a forward-thinking, strong, respected senior mainframe specialist support the team with education and coaching.

The bottom line on talent

Transformation requires people. If staffing concerns are driving your platform decisions, fix the staffing problem first; it is faster and cheaper than replacing an entire platform. And if you are planning to migrate away from mainframes, remember: you will need mainframe expertise throughout that multi-year journey anyway.

The talent is available. You just need to make the work visible, modern, and appealing. When you do that, the applications will come.

Chapter 18 The future of mainframe computing

We have seen that mainframes are not synonymous with legacy, and legacy does not necessarily mean outdated. Instead, the mainframe serves as an evolutionary platform in the middle, sometimes leading modern technological developments, such as AI, ransomware resilience, and quantum-safe security. Therefore, as platform users, we should not treat the mainframe as such; instead, we should invest in innovating the applications and infrastructure, just as we do for all other parts of the IT landscape.

In a modern IT landscape, the mainframe is well-suited to securely and robustly handle high-volume transaction workloads. As such, it is a perfect backbone in hybrid IT ecosystems.

The modern mainframe is not a paradox

In this book, I have provided an overview of the mainframe, including its origins and future. Today, the mainframe runs 70% of the world's transactions. Its reliability, security, and scalability are unparalleled in the IT industry.

We see frontrunning organizations that effectively integrate cloud-native front-office and mid-office applications operating in the public cloud with robust mainframe applications on-premise. These organizations utilize COBOL applications, benefiting from decades of investment in a modernized, enhanced portfolio that includes newly developed applications written in Java and Python. These new applications are deployed natively on z/OS and in OpenShift-managed Linux containers on IBM Z.

So, back to that question from the beginning: Should you keep it? Modernize it? Replace it? By now, you have the information you need to decide. But whatever you choose, remember: doing nothing is still the only wrong answer. Here's what the future looks like for those who choose to invest.

Strategic pillars for the future of the mainframe

I see several pillars essential for the mainframe of the future.

Hybrid architecture

The future of the mainframe is as a platform that typically hosts system-of-record applications integrated with cloud technologies, cloud applications, AI, and quantum technologies. Cloud integrations are achieved by closely following modern open-source integration technologies. Support for REST APIs has long existed and should be further streamlined. More modern technologies, such as Kafka and Pulsar, as well as others like native AI integration solutions, are emerging and can run on z/OS while integrated with mainframe applications.

IBM is developing a mainframe server equipped with integrated AI chips for AI inferencing and large language models with the Telum and Spyre technologies. These technologies enhance the platform with features that allow the IBM Z server to serve as a backbone for enterprise AI capabilities.

While IBM is also a leader in the development of Quantum technology, the IBM Z mainframe platform is a strategic, classic computer ideally positioned to integrate Quantum-based functions with classic (non-Quantum) applications.

Case Study: high-performance AI fraud detection with mainframe and cloud technologies

In Figure 63, you can see a solution overview from a financial sector organization that built a high-performing fraud-detection system by leveraging mainframe AI and cloud-native technologies.

The fraud detection models were developed and trained in the cloud, taking advantage of its scalability and advanced AI/ML tooling. To achieve the required real-time performance, the trained models were deployed close to the core payment systems on z/OS, within an OpenShift cluster on the mainframe. This hybrid approach combined the strengths of cloud-based innovation with the mainframe's low-latency, high-throughput capabilities.

The system easily exceeded the Service Level Agreement (SLA) target, achieving more than 5000 transactions per second with latency below 5 milliseconds.

This solution also enabled the organization to innovate with a new, homegrown AI-driven solution and to deliver a next-generation fraud detection service.

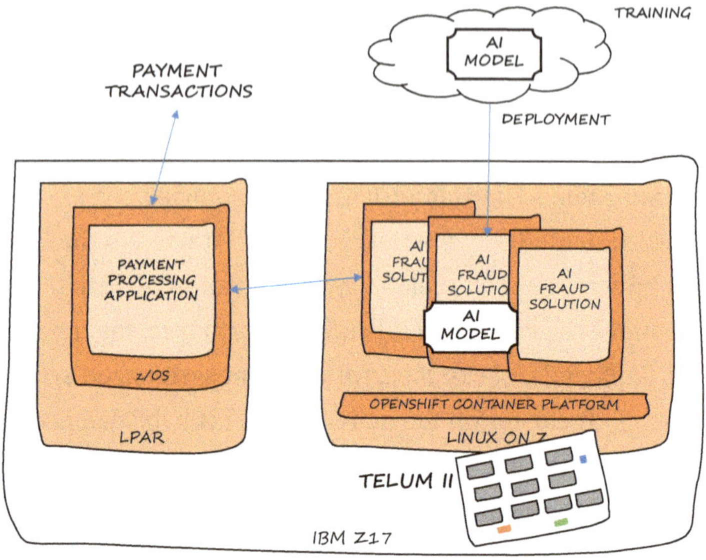

Figure 63 Hybrid AI solution for AI fraud detection in IBM Z

AI and automation

GenAI-supported development, operations, and IT optimization have become standard practice. Tools like IBM watsonx enhance the entire development lifecycle for all programming activities on the mainframe platform.

Monitoring tools are equipped with integrated AI capabilities. Technologies such as AI-assisted Db2 query optimization and workload management are becoming standard. AI will automatically handle numerous operational adjustments and offer operations teams suggestions for preventing and resolving incidents.

Generative AI keeps applications up to date and will help create self-healing systems. AI helps optimize critical business processes, such as critical batch processing.

Quantum-Safe Infrastructure and pervasive encryption

Mainframes were among the first to facilitate quantum-safe encryption. Today, pervasive encryption is the norm; all data is encrypted, whether in flight in networking components, stored on storage, or in memory.

Quantum-safe encryption is integrated with pervasive encryption to protect data on the mainframe against current and future threats.

Developer Experience (DevX) Revolution

The mainframe platform leverages state-of-the-art development practices. The same tools used for mainframe development apply to other contemporary computing platforms. Developers enjoy a consistent, intuitive experience, whether they are writing COBOL, Python, Java, Go, or another programming language, as well as in infrastructure and code specifications like YAML, Ansible playbooks, Terraform, or any future technology. Common tools and processes simplify developers' switching between languages. Application developers have the same experience as infrastructure code developers.

Application testing and debugging are part of the developer experience. Developer tools assist in creating, running, and evaluating test scenarios across all testing types.

Generative AI supports all aspects of development, from coding and quality validation to testing and performance evaluation, as well as documentation generation.

The shift towards a cloud-native development style continues. This style masks many infrastructure aspects from developers, giving them instant access to scalable resources.

The consumable mainframe

The mainframe platform offers a cloud-like self-service experience for managing infrastructure and applications. It empowers developers by eliminating the complexities of traditional infrastructure management.

Development teams can autonomously provision and manage the necessary application and infrastructure resources using predefined templates and guidelines through the self-service platform.

Software suppliers for the mainframe deliver a consistent software installation and lifecycle management experience, similar to standard practice on other platforms. The infrastructure team can retrieve the necessary software packages from a software repository. With a container-management approach, the lifecycle of all infrastructure components can be effectively managed.

Challenges and opportunities

Overcoming IBM Z inertia

A significant challenge for many organizations using a mainframe is overcoming IBM Z inertia. While Broadcom, Rocket Software, IBM, and other organizations offer numerous platforms for learning about the mainframe, many companies fail to take advantage of these resources. Instead, they continue to rely on aging staff, like ostriches with their heads in the sand, ignoring the need for innovation and modernization.

To address this, organizations should focus on attracting young IT talent through innovative tools and initiatives. Hackathons, talent contests, and gamified assessments like IBM Z Xplore can make the mainframe platform appealing to a new generation of IT professionals. These young professionals, trained in the latest technologies, including AI, modern development tools, and agile methodologies, can bring fresh perspectives and help modernize your organization's platform.

Invest in innovation, not just maintenance

It's critical to invest in the mainframe platform, not just maintain it. Allocate a portion of your innovation budget to modernizing the mainframe, ensuring it remains a strategic asset rather than a legacy burden. This investment will help bridge the gap between traditional mainframe expertise and modern IT practices.

Foster collaboration and open-source participation

Encourage participation in open-source projects related to the mainframe platform. Open-source communities are hubs where modern IT professionals collaborate, innovate, and share knowledge. By fostering involvement in these projects, organizations can attract new talent, accelerate innovation, and ensure the mainframe remains relevant in today's fast-evolving technology landscape.

Additionally, promote active engagement in forums, discussion boards, and collaborative platforms like Discord, Slack, or GitHub. These platforms provide opportunities for mainframe professionals to connect, exchange ideas, and collectively solve challenges. Building a vibrant community around the mainframe will help bridge the gap between traditional expertise and modern IT practices, ensuring the platform continues to evolve and thrive.

Improving accessibility to the platform

Another challenge is access to the platform, which is crucial for hands-on learning and experimentation. Programs like IBM Z Explore and Broadcom's Mainframe Vitality Program provide students and professionals with access to mainframe environments for learning and experimentation. However, accessibility could be further improved.

We should aim to build a collaborative, open-source culture for the mainframe, where experimentation is encouraged, and projects can be easily shared on platforms like GitHub. While not everyone can have a "mainframe laptop," we can explore ways to provide broader access to real mainframe platforms, perhaps through limited-use, cloud-based environments or nominal-fee services. IBM and other software vendors should think creatively about how to make such "playgrounds" accessible, recognizing their potential to foster innovation and attract new talent to the mainframe ecosystem.

Lindy's Law in the Age of Mainframes

Lindy's Law teaches us that the longer a technology survives, the more likely it is to endure. Now in its seventh decade, the mainframe is not just surviving but thriving. Like Rome's aqueducts or the printed book, its longevity is not accidental. It demonstrates a timeless truth: systems that adapt without sacrificing their core purpose outlive revolutions.

The mainframe's secret isn't a longing for the past but mastery of a paradox: stability fuels evolution. While others pursue disruption, it provides something rarer: *dependable transformation*. It resembles a city: it never sleeps yet constantly rebuilds its infrastructure without shutting down. That's the mainframe.

In a world where "legacy" is a slur, it is better to reframe it. The mainframe isn't resisting the future; it is *redefining resilience*. The benefits of new IT are assimilated; cloud technologies are integrated, as is AI technology, while auditing for hallucinations, and Quantum is gracefully anticipated. By doing so, the mainframe benefits from disorder. It is antifragile.

The endgame isn't retirement; it's renewal.

The next chapter isn't about survival; it's about *sovereignty*.

So, to the disruptors: the mainframe has outlasted your grandparents' technology and will likely outlast yours.

To the skeptics: the code that powered the moon landing now also powers your mortgage. What makes you think it can't power Mars?

The future isn't built by erasing history but by layering it. The mainframe's next layer starts now.

Your turn.

Enjoy the journey.

About the Author

Niek de Greef has worked with mainframe systems since 1990, guiding organizations through strategic technology transformations. As Lead Architect Enterprise Systems at a major European bank, he leads mainframe architecture strategy and teams defining enterprise roadmaps for one of Europe's largest financial institutions.

Through his consultancy work with IBM and his own company Seneqa, Niek has advised Fortune 500 companies across Europe and Asia on mainframe modernization. His engagements span platform strategy for major insurers, transformation projects in international banking, and solutions for high-volume transaction-processing environments.

Previously, as an Executive IT Architect at IBM, he served as a Global Account Architect and co-authored several IBM Redbooks. He holds a Master's degree in Computer Science from the University of Twente, an MBA from Henley Management College, and is a certified Distinguished Chief Architect.

What distinguishes Niek's approach is his focus on strategic confidence rather than technical complexity. Having witnessed executives struggle with mainframe decisions, he developed practical frameworks that translate technical realities into clear business choices.

"Too many smart leaders avoid mainframe decisions because they feel overwhelmed by technical complexity," he explains. "This book helps executives make confident strategic choices based on business value, not technical fear."

Connect with Niek de Greef:

Professional consulting: seneqa.nl

Strategic insights: execpgm.org

Acknowledgments

Heartfelt thanks to Erik Bakker, Ralph van Beek, Leendert Blondeel, Georges de Boeck, Henk van Dasler, Erwin Klaus, Martijn Raave, and Satya Srungarapu for their invaluable encouragement, reviews, and insightful suggestions that sharpened this book. (Special nod to Georges for debugging my HelloWorld Java program, saving me from eternal embarrassment.)

Gratitude to colleagues across my employers ING, CTG, IBM, and especially those at Rabobank over the most recent decade; the many worldwide clients I've consulted for and software/service companies I have worked with including IBM, Broadcom, Kyndryl, BMC, Rocket Software, ICU IT Services, ACI, and others, whose decades of collaboration and generous knowledge-sharing infused these pages with hard-won wisdom.

Appreciation to the mainframe community: SHARE, GSE, GS UK, and GS NL events; IBM Z forums; and thought leaders whose blogs and talks sparked key ideas.

To my family, for their enduring patience during long evenings, nights, and weekend absences.

Finally, to the next generation of mainframe innovators: may this book light your path.

Glossary

A

ACF2 (Access Control Facility 2)
A security management product from Broadcom that implements the System Authorization Facility (SAF) interface, competing with IBM RACF.

Adabas
A database management system from Software AG that uses an inverted list data model. Often used with the Natural programming language.

Address Space
The z/OS equivalent of a process in Unix or Windows. Each address space provides a programme with its own protected memory space for execution.

Agile
A software development methodology emphasising iterative development, collaboration, and flexibility in responding to change.

AI Accelerator
Specialised hardware (Telum, Spyre) designed to enhance AI processing capabilities on IBM Z servers, enabling inference and machine learning workloads.

ALIAS
An entry in the master catalogue that directs z/OS to look in a specific user catalogue for datasets with particular name patterns.

Ansible
An open-source automation tool for infrastructure provisioning, configuration management, and application deployment.

API (Application Programming Interface)
A set of protocols and tools for building software applications, allowing different programs to communicate with each other.

Application Server

Middleware that provides a runtime environment for applications, handling communication, transactions, database connectivity, and other common functions.

ASCII (American Standard Code for Information Interchange)

The character encoding system used on most non-mainframe computers is different from EBCDIC, which is used on mainframes.

Assembler

A low-level programming language that directly controls CPU instructions. Whilst extremely fast, it's difficult to maintain, and skills are increasingly scarce.

B

BASE24

A banking transaction processing application from ACI Worldwide, available on z/OS and other platforms.

Batch Processing

A method of running programmes that process large volumes of data without user interaction, typically scheduled to run at specific times.

Batch Window

The time period allocated for running batch jobs, often overnight when online transaction volumes are lower.

BMC

A software company providing mainframe tools, including MainView (monitoring), Control-M (job scheduling), and various automation products.

Broadcom

A major mainframe software vendor owning products including CA-1, CA-7, Datacom, IDMS, Endevor, and various management tools.

Build

A complete package of application artifacts (programmes, scripts, configuration files) ready for deployment to a runtime environment.

Business Logic

The part of an application that implements business rules and processes, separate from presentation and data access layers.

C

CA7

A job scheduling product from Broadcom (formerly Computer Associates), used to automate and manage batch processing workflows.

Capacity Planning

The process of determining computing resources needed to meet current and future business demands.

Catalogue

A z/OS dataset that maintains an index of other datasets and their locations on disk volumes. Similar to a directory structure in Unix/Windows.

CI/CD (Continuous Integration/Continuous Deployment)

Automated practices for frequently integrating code changes and deploying them to production environments.

CICS (Customer Information Control System)

IBM's transaction manager and application server for z/OS, supporting high-volume transaction processing in COBOL, PL/I, and Java.

CICSPlex

A configuration of multiple CICS regions working together in a Parallel Sysplex, providing high availability and scalability.

CLIST

An older z/OS scripting language, largely superseded by Rexx for automation tasks.

Cloud

Computing resources delivered as a service over the internet, including infrastructure (IaaS), platforms (PaaS), and software (SaaS).

COBOL (Common Business-Oriented Language)

A business-oriented programming language developed in 1959, it is still widely used on mainframes for its readability and performance.

Compiler

A programme that translates source code into executable machine instructions (load modules).

Container

See Linux Container.

Coupling Facility

A specialised component in a Parallel Sysplex that provides shared memory and communication facilities for z/OS cluster members.

CPU (Central Processing Unit)

The processor core that executes instructions. Mainframes can have hundreds of CPU cores.

Cryptography

The practice of securing information through encryption, with mainframes providing hardware-accelerated cryptographic capabilities.

Cybervault

IBM's solution for creating immutable backups of mainframe data, protecting against ransomware and malicious attacks.

Cylinder

An obsolete measurement of disk storage capacity from rotating disk technology, still referenced in z/OS dataset definitions for historical reasons.

D

DASD (Direct Access Storage Device)

Traditional mainframe terminology for disk storage, though modern systems use solid-state drives rather than spinning disks.

Data Sharing Group

A Db2 configuration allowing multiple Db2 subsystems to share access to the same data across a Parallel Sysplex.

Dataset

The z/OS term for a file. Datasets are record-oriented and can have different structures (sequential, VSAM).

Datacom/DB

A relational database management system from Broadcom, often used with the IDEAL development environment.

Db2

IBM's relational database management system for z/OS organizes data in tables and supports SQL queries.

DB2 for z/OS

See Db2.

Deployment

The process of installing and configuring software in a runtime environment.

DevOps

A methodology combining software development (Dev) and IT operations (Ops) to shorten development cycles and improve deployment frequency.

Disaster Recovery

Procedures and technologies for recovering IT systems and data after catastrophic failures or disasters.

DL/I (Data Language/I)

The language used to access and manipulate data in IMS hierarchical databases.

Docker

A platform for developing and running containerised applications, with container support on z/OS through zCX and Linux on Z.

Drawer

The mainframe equivalent of a motherboard, housing CPU chips, memory, and other components.

Dynatrace

An application performance monitoring tool that provides observability across distributed systems, including mainframes.

E

Easytrieve

A programming language from Broadcom used for ad hoc reporting and data processing on z/OS.

EBCDIC (Extended Binary Coded Decimal Interchange Code)

The character encoding system used on mainframes, different from the ASCII system used on most other computers.

Eclipse

An open-source integrated development environment (IDE) used as the basis for z/OS development tools, such as z/OS Explorer.

Encryption

The process of encoding data to prevent unauthorised access, with mainframes offering hardware-accelerated encryption capabilities.

Endevor

A source code management tool from Broadcom for z/OS development, supporting staged software lifecycle processes.

Enterprise Service Bus (ESB)

Integration middleware that enables communication between different applications using various protocols and message formats.

Exit Point

A customisation interface in z/OS or middleware that allows users to insert their own code to modify system behaviour.

F

FICON (Fibre Connection)

The proprietary protocol used by mainframes to connect to storage systems over fibre-optic networks.

File Transfer Protocol (FTP)

A standard protocol for transferring files between systems, supported on z/OS with secure variants like SFTP.

Flex Capacity

IBM licensing models that provide more flexible pricing based on actual usage patterns rather than fixed capacity entitlements.

Fortran

A programming language designed for scientific and engineering calculations, still available on z/OS.

G

GDPS (Geographically Dispersed Parallel Sysplex)

An extension of Parallel Sysplex that provides data mirroring and automatic failover between geographically separated data centres.

General-Purpose CPU

A standard CPU used for traditional mainframe workloads, such as COBOL and PL/I applications.

Generative AI

Artificial intelligence systems that can generate new content, increasingly used for code generation and development assistance on mainframes.

Git

A distributed version control system widely used for source code management, now supporting z/OS development.

GitHub

A cloud-based platform for Git repositories, supporting collaboration and version control for mainframe and other development.

Grafana

An open-source platform for monitoring and observability, capable of visualising mainframe metrics alongside other systems.

Green Screen

Colloquial term for 3270 terminal interfaces, referring to the green text on black background displays used historically.

H

Hardware MSU

The raw computing capacity of a mainframe as it comes from the factory, distinct from the Software MSU used for licensing.

High Availability

System design ensuring continuous operation with minimal downtime, a key strength of mainframe architecture.

Hybrid Cloud

An IT architecture combining on-premise systems (often including mainframes) with public cloud services.

Hypervisor

Software that creates and manages virtual machines. z/VM and KVM are hypervisors for IBM Z.

I

IBM Z

IBM's current branding for its mainframe hardware platform encompassing z14, z15, z16, z17, and future generations.

IDAA (IBM Db2 Analytics Accelerator)

A specialised appliance that offloads complex analytical queries from Db2 for z/OS to improve performance.

IDEAL

A fourth-generation programming language from Broadcom, designed for use with Datacom/DB.

IDMS

A transaction manager and network database system from Broadcom, consisting of IDMS/DC and IDMS/DB components.

IFL (Integrated Facility for Linux)

A specialty engine CPU configured exclusively for running Linux workloads on IBM Z.

IMS (Information Management System)

IBM's transaction manager (IMS/TM) and hierarchical database (IMS/DB), originally developed for NASA's Apollo programme.

Infrastructure as Code

The practice of managing and provisioning infrastructure through machine-readable definition files rather than manual configuration.

Integration

The process of connecting different applications and systems to work together, using various technologies and patterns.

Internal Reader

The z/OS component that accepts JCL for job submission, replacing the historical punch card readers.

ISPF (Interactive System Productivity Facility)

A menu-driven interface for z/OS that provides editing, dataset management, and other utilities. Built on top of TSO.

ISPW

A source code management and development tool from BMC (formerly Compuware), supporting modern DevOps practices for mainframes.

J

Java

An object-oriented programming language that runs on the Java Virtual Machine (JVM), supported on z/OS, including on zIIP processors.

JCL (Job Control Language)
The scripting language used to define and execute batch jobs on z/OS, with syntax dating back to the punch card era.

JDBC/ODBC
Standard database connectivity protocols (Java Database Connectivity / Open Database Connectivity) allowing applications to access databases.

Jenkins
An open-source automation server supporting CI/CD pipelines, increasingly used for mainframe application development.

Job
A unit of work submitted to z/OS for processing, defined by JCL and executed in batch mode.

Job Scheduler
Software that automates the execution and management of batch jobs based on schedules, dependencies, and conditions.

JSON (JavaScript Object Notation)
A lightweight data format commonly used in REST APIs and modern application integration.

JVM (Java Virtual Machine)
The runtime environment that executes Java programs, available on z/OS for both traditional and zIIP processors.

K

Kafka
An open-source event streaming platform that enables applications to publish and subscribe to data events in real-time.

KVM (Kernel-based Virtual Machine)

An open-source hypervisor that can run on IBM Z, providing virtualisation for Linux instances.

Kubernetes

An open-source platform for automating deployment, scaling, and management of containerised applications.

L

Legacy

Older technology or applications, though often misapplied to mainframes, which support modern capabilities when properly maintained.

Liberty

See WebSphere Liberty.

Lindy's Law

The theory that the future life expectancy of non-perishable things is proportional to their current age, often applied to mainframe longevity.

Linux Container

A lightweight, portable package combining an application and its dependencies, enabling consistent deployment across environments.

Linux on IBM Z

Linux distributions (Red Hat, SUSE, Ubuntu) ported to run on IBM Z hardware, also called zLinux.

Load Module

The compiled, executable version of a programme, ready to run on z/OS.

LPAR (Logical Partition)

A virtualised server environment created by dividing mainframe hardware into isolated sections, each running its own operating system.

M

Mainframe

A large, central computer designed to run multiple computing tasks simultaneously in a stable and secure manner.

Managed File Transfer (MFT)

Specialised software for secure, reliable file exchange with features like encryption, automation, and detailed auditing.

Master Catalog

The primary catalog in z/OS, containing references to system datasets and aliases pointing to user catalogues.

Maven

A build automation tool primarily for Java projects, increasingly used in mainframe development workflows.

Microservices

An architectural style structuring applications as collections of loosely coupled, independently deployable services.

Middleware

Software that sits between the operating system and applications, providing common services like transaction processing and messaging.

MIPS (Million Instructions Per Second)

A measure of computing performance used on non-mainframe platforms, similar to MSU on mainframes.

MLC (Monthly License Charge)

A software licensing model where customers pay a variable monthly fee based on actual CPU usage (measured in MSUs).

Modernisation

The process of updating legacy systems with current technologies, architectures, and development practices.

Monitoring

The continuous observation of system and application health, performance, and security status.

MQ

See WebSphere MQ.

MSU (Million Service Units)

The unit of measurement for mainframe computing capacity, used to calculate software licensing costs.

Multifactor Authentication (MFA)

A security method requiring users to provide two or more verification factors to access systems.

MVS (Multiple Virtual Storage)

The predecessor to z/OS, developed in the 1970s. The core technology remains in modern z/OS.

N

Natural

Software AG's fourth-generation programming language, designed for developing applications with the Adabas database.

Network Database

A database model where records are connected in a network structure, used by systems like IDMS/DB.

O

Observability

The ability to understand system internal states from external outputs, using metrics, logs, and traces.

OpenShift

Red Hat's Kubernetes-based container platform for deploying and managing containerised applications at scale.

OpenTelemetry

An open-source framework for generating, collecting, and exporting telemetry data (metrics, logs, traces) from applications.

Operating System

The fundamental software managing hardware resources and providing services for application programs.

OTC (One-Time Charge)

A perpetual software license model where customers pay once for unlimited use up to a specified capacity.

P

Parallel Sysplex

A z/OS clustering technology that combines multiple z/OS instances across multiple servers into a single logical system.

PCIe (Peripheral Component Interconnect Express)

A standard interface for connecting hardware components, used in mainframes for I/O cards and other devices.

Performance

The measure of system responsiveness, throughput, and resource utilisation under various workloads.

Pervasive Encryption

A mainframe security feature that encrypts all data by default: at rest, in transit, and in memory.

PL/I (Programming Language One)

A programming language developed in the 1960s for both business and scientific applications on mainframes.

POSIX (Portable Operating System Interface)
A family of standards for Unix-like operating systems, supported by z/OS Unix System Services.
PR/SM (Processor Resource/Systems Manager)
The mainframe's built-in tool for creating logical partitions (LPARs), dividing hardware into smaller virtual servers.
Python
A popular high-level programming language, increasingly supported on z/OS for scripting, automation, and application development.

Q

Quantum Computing
An emerging technology using quantum mechanics for computation, with IBM developing integration between quantum systems and mainframes.
Queue Sharing Group
A configuration allowing multiple MQ queue managers to share the same message queues across a Parallel Sysplex.

R

RACF (Resource Access Control Facility)
IBM's security management product that implements the System Authorization Facility (SAF) interface.
Ransomware
Malicious software that encrypts data and demands payment for restoration, mitigated on mainframes through Cybervault and other protections.

Refactoring

The process of restructuring existing code or applications without changing external behaviour, often to improve maintainability.

Rehosting

Migrating applications to a different infrastructure whilst maintaining the same application code and middleware stack.

Relational Database

A database organized in tables with relationships between them, using SQL for queries. Examples include Db2 and Datacom/DB.

REST (Representational State Transfer)

A modern architectural style for web services, typically using JSON for lightweight API communication.

Rexx

A scripting language used on z/OS for automation tasks, similar to shell scripts in Unix.

Rocket Software

A software company providing mainframe tools and supporting various legacy products acquired from other vendors.

S

SAF (System Authorization Facility)

z/OS's centralised security interface that provides authentication and authorisation functions.

SAN (Storage Area Network)

A specialised high-speed network connecting servers to storage devices.

SAS

A programming language and analytics platform widely used on mainframes for data analysis and reporting.

Scalability

The ability of a system to handle growing workloads by adding resources, a key strength of mainframe architecture.

SCLM (Software Configuration and Library Manager)

IBM's discontinued source code management tool for z/OS, replaced by modern alternatives like Git.

SDSF (System Display and Search Facility)

An IBM product providing system operators with tools to monitor and manage z/OS processes and output.

Security

The protection of systems and data from unauthorised access, use, disclosure, disruption, or destruction.

Sequential Dataset

A dataset organized linearly from first record to last, similar to a text file in Unix/Windows.

Service Unit (SU)

A measure of computing work on a mainframe, calculated based on CPU instructions processed. A million service units equals one MSU.

SFTP (Secure File Transfer Protocol)

An encrypted version of FTP for secure file transfers between systems.

Silo

An isolated application or system with limited integration with other systems, considered an anti-pattern in modern architecture.

SMF (System Management Facility)

z/OS's built-in facility for logging system events and collecting performance data.

SOAP (Simple Object Access Protocol)

An older web services protocol using XML for structured message exchange between applications.

Software AG

A software company providing mainframe products, including Adabas, Natural, and various integration tools.

Software MSU

The capacity metric used to calculate software licensing costs, derived from but different than hardware MSU.

Source Code Management (SCM)

Systems for tracking and managing changes to source code, such as Git, Endevor, or ISPW.

Specialty Engine

A mainframe CPU configured for specific workloads (zIIP, IFL, ICF, SAP) to reduce software licensing costs.

Splunk

An observability platform for searching, monitoring, and analysing machine-generated data, supporting mainframe integration.

Spyre

IBM's AI accelerator card for intensive machine learning workloads on IBM Z, supporting Large Language Model and complex inferencing.

SQL (Structured Query Language)

The standard language for interacting with relational databases like Db2 and Datacom/DB.

SSD (Solid State Drive)

Modern storage technology using flash memory, replacing spinning disks in mainframe storage systems.

Sysplex

Short for Parallel Sysplex, a cluster of z/OS systems working together as a single logical system.

System Log

The central repository in z/OS where all system messages, warnings, and errors are recorded.

System of Record

The authoritative source for specific business data, often hosted on mainframes for critical business information.

T

Tape

Magnetic tape storage used for backups and archives, still in use in some organizations as a cost-effective long-term retention.

TCO (Total Cost of Ownership)

The complete cost of acquiring, implementing, operating, and maintaining a technology platform over its lifetime.

Technical Debt

The accumulated cost of deferred maintenance, outdated components, and architectural shortcuts in IT systems.

Telnet

A network protocol for remote terminal access, largely superseded by SSH for security reasons.

Telum

IBM's integrated AI processor built into z16 and later mainframe CPUs, enabling real-time AI inference during transaction processing.

Terraform

An infrastructure-as-code tool for provisioning and managing infrastructure across multiple platforms.

3270 Terminal

The terminal technology developed for mainframes in the 1960s, now largely replaced by software emulation. Origin of "green screen."

Top Secret

A security management product from Broadcom implementing the System Authorization Facility (SAF) interface.

Topaz

A suite of development tools from BMC (formerly Compuware) for mainframe application development and testing.

Transaction

A unit of work in an application, typically an atomic operation that either completes entirely or fails completely.

Transaction Manager

See Application Server. The traditional mainframe term for what's now called an application server.

Transformation

The process of fundamentally changing applications or systems to align with modern architectures and practices.

TSO (Time Sharing Option)

z/OS's interactive command-line interface, similar to a Unix shell or Windows command prompt.

U

Unicode

A modern character encoding standard supporting characters from all writing systems, increasingly used on mainframes.

Unix

A family of operating systems, with z/OS Unix System Services providing Unix compatibility on mainframes.

User Catalog

A catalog containing entries for application and user datasets, referenced by an alias in the master catalog.

V

Virtual Machine

An emulated computer system running on physical hardware, created by hypervisors like z/VM or KVM.

Virtual Storage

The z/OS term for memory (RAM). Often confusing because "storage" elsewhere typically means disk space.

Visual Studio Code

A popular code editor from Microsoft, now supporting z/OS development through extensions like IBM Z Open Editor.

VSAM (Virtual Storage Access Method)

A dataset organization method using an indexed structure for high-speed direct access to records by key value.

W

Waterfall

A sequential software development methodology where each phase must complete before the next begins. Contrasts with agile methods.

WebSphere Application Server

IBM's Java EE (Jakarta EE) compliant application server, available on z/OS and other platforms.

WebSphere Liberty

IBM's lightweight, modular alternative to traditional WebSphere Application Server, optimized for cloud-native development.

WebSphere MQ

IBM's messaging middleware for asynchronous communication between applications, now called IBM MQ.

Workload

The collection of tasks and programmes running on a system, often categorised as batch, online, or analytical.

X

x86

The processor architecture used in most PC and server hardware, different from IBM's z/Architecture used in mainframes.

XML (Extensible Markup Language)

A structured data format used in SOAP web services and configuration files.

Z

z/Architecture

IBM's 64-bit processor architecture for mainframe CPUs, distinct from Intel's x86 architecture.

zCX (z/OS Container Extensions)

Technology allowing Linux containers to run within the z/OS operating system as z/OS address spaces.

zIIP (System z Integrated Information Processor)

A specialty engine for running Java, certain Db2 functions, and other eligible workloads at reduced software cost.

z/OS

IBM's flagship mainframe operating system, evolved from MVS. Combines traditional MVS functionality with Unix capabilities.

z/OS Connect

IBM's tool for creating REST APIs from mainframe applications and enabling z/OS applications to call external REST services.

z/OS Explorer

An Eclipse-based desktop tool for z/OS development and system management with a modern graphical interface.

z/OS Unix System Services (z/OS Unix)

The Unix-compliant component of z/OS, providing POSIX-standard functionality and a Unix shell environment.

Zowe

An open-source framework providing modern interfaces and tools for z/OS development, operations, and integration.

z/TPF (Transaction Processing Facility)

A specialised real-time operating system for IBM Z, used for high-volume, low-latency transaction processing.

z/VM

A hypervisor operating system for IBM Z, creating virtual machines. Considered "the mother of all hypervisors."

z/VSE

A smaller-scale mainframe operating system, the "little brother" of z/OS, with fewer features but lower overhead.

Appendix A: Assessment Frameworks

These frameworks align with the concepts discussed throughout this book. Use them to evaluate your mainframe platform and guide strategic decisions.

Framework 0: The "Pre-Flight Check"

CRITICAL SIGNAL	YES	NO
1 - Software out of support for >2 years?	☐	☐
2 - Key staff retiring within 2 years with no succession plan?	☐	☐
3 - Platform upgrades postponed for >5 yrs?	☐	☐
4. Platform actively blocking business innovation	☐	☐
5. Unable to calculate total cost of ownership	☐	☐

Your Score:

- 0 Yes: You have time to plan strategically → Use Frameworks 1 & 2
- 1-2 Yes: Begin assessment within 3 months → Complete all frameworks
- 3+ Yes: This is urgent → Get external help NOW while doing assessment

Framework 1: Mainframe Platform Health Assessment

This framework helps you assess the current state of your mainframe platform across the key dimensions discussed in Chapters 13 and 17.

How to Use This Framework

Work through each section with your technical and business teams. Score each area honestly. The goal isn't to achieve a perfect score but to identify where you need to focus your efforts.

Scoring Guide:

5 - Excellent: Modern, well-maintained, aligned with best practices

3 - Adequate: Functional but showing age, some technical debt

1 - Critical: Significant risk, urgent attention needed

N/A: Not applicable to your organization

Section A: Technical Vitality

Based on the technical debt discussion in Chapter 13.

Area	Score (1-5)	Notes
Programming Languages		
No Assembler in business applications	☐	See Ch 7
Programs compiled in the last 5 years	☐	
Using supported languages only	☐	
Modern languages (Java/Python) adopted	☐	
Infrastructure		
z/OS version within IBM support window	☐	See Ch 4
Middleware versions current (within two releases)	☐	See Ch 6
No unsupported software in production	☐	
Hardware within two generations of current	☐	See Ch 3
Customizations		
Limited use of z/OS exits (< 10 active)	☐	See Ch 13
No home-grown middleware	☐	
Exit points documented and maintained	☐	

Section A Score: ____ / 55 (or applicable total)

Red Flags (Circle any that apply):

Assembler programs with no maintainers

Software out of support for > 2 years

Programs not compiled in > 10 years

Undocumented exits in critical paths

Section B: Development & Operations Maturity

Based on the DevOps discussion in Chapter 9.

Area	Score (1-5)	Notes
Source Code Management		
All code in modern SCM (Git, etc.)	☐	See Ch 9
Version control for all artifacts	☐	
Branching strategy defined	☐	
Build & Deployment		
Automated build process	☐	
Automated deployment to test	☐	
Automated deployment to production	☐	
Builds are environment-agnostic	☐	
Development Process		
Agile methodology in use	☐	
CI/CD pipeline operational	☐	
Automated testing in place	☐	
Mean time to deploy < 1 week	☐	
Tools & Environment		
Modern IDEs available (VS Code, Eclipse)	☐	See Ch 5
Developers use modern tools	☐	
Self-service environment provisioning	☐	

Section B Score: ____ / 70 (or applicable total)

Red Flags (Circle any that apply):

Still using waterfall exclusively

Manual deployments only

Changes take > 1 month to production

No automated testing

Section C: Application Architecture

Based on the modern architecture discussion in Chapter 12.

Area	Score (1-5)	Notes
Layering		
Clear separation: presentation/business/data	☐	See Ch 12
Business logic reusable	☐	
No presentation logic in mainframe apps	☐	
Integration		
Service-oriented interfaces	☐	
REST APIs available	☐	See Ch 8
No direct database access between apps	☐	
Modern integration patterns used	☐	
Technical Design		
Applications use modern middleware	☐	See Ch 6
Minimal screen-scraping solutions	☐	
Data owned by applications	☐	
Limited use of VSAM (< 10% of data)	☐	See Ch 5

Section C Score: ____ / 60 (or applicable total)

Red Flags (Circle any that apply):

Monolithic silo applications

Heavy use of screen scraping

Direct database access between apps

No API strategy

Framework 2: Transformation Decision Matrix

This framework helps you decide whether to modernize or migrate your mainframe applications. Based on Chapter 13.

Step 1: Assess Each Application

For each major application, evaluate:

Criterion	Score (1-5)	Weight	Weighted Score
Business Value			
Revenue/cost impact	☐	3	☐
Strategic importance	☐	3	☐
Customer/user satisfaction	☐	2	☐
Technical Health			
Code quality	☐	2	☐
Documentation quality	☐	1	☐
Use of modern practices	☐	2	☐
Change Frequency			
Business changes needed	☐	2	☐
Regulatory changes needed	☐	2	☐
Skills			
Available expertise	☐	2	☐
Knowledge transfer done	☐	2	☐

Total Weighted Score: ____ / 105

Step 2: Map to Strategy

Plot your applications on this matrix:

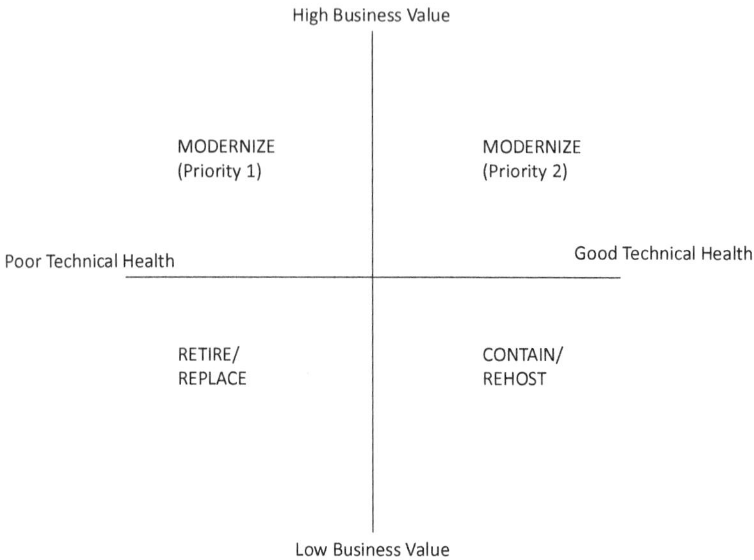

Scoring Guide:

Technical Health: Score from Step 1, sections 2-4

Business Value: Score from Step 1, section 1

Strategy Recommendations:

Modernize Priority 1 (High value, Poor health)

These applications are critical but struggling. Invest in:

Refactoring critical paths

Adding REST APIs

Updating architecture

See Chapter 12 for patterns

Modernize Priority 2 (High value, Good health)
These are your success stories. Focus on:
Continuous improvement
Modern DevOps practices
Integration with new technologies
See Chapter 9

Retire/Replace (Low value, Poor health)
These applications consume resources without delivering value:
Evaluate off-the-shelf alternatives
Consider consolidation
Plan for retirement
See Chapter 13

Contain/Rehost (Low value, Good health)
These work but aren't strategic:
Minimize investment
Consider rehosting if cost-effective
Maintain but don't enhance
See Chapter 13

A Final Word

These frameworks are tools, not gospel. Adapt them to your organization's specific context. The goal is to replace gut feelings with informed decisions whilst maintaining the flexibility to adjust as you learn.

As I said in multiple places, doing nothing is not an option. Use these frameworks to understand where you stand, then decide where you need to go.

The rest is execution.

www.ingramcontent.com/pod-product-compliance
Lightning Source LLC
Chambersburg PA
CBHW062308240926
51846CB00013B/671
9789083597003